Jim Poling Sr.

Jim Poling Sr. was a newspaper journalist for thirty-five years before turning to freelance magazine and book writing. Much of his journalism career was spent with the national news agency Canadian Press. His postings there included Edmonton, Ottawa, Vancouver, and Toronto, as well as assignments across the Far North, Alaska, Russia, Scandinavia, and Cuba. He began his CP career as a reporter and worked as editor, bureau chief, editor-in-chief, and general manager.

Jim is also the author of *Waking Nanabijou*, a memoir about his search for his mother's origins and an exploration of the shameful ongoing discrimination against First Nations people. His other books include *Tom Thomson: The Life and Death of the Famous Canadian Painter* and *The Canoe: An Illustrated History*. Jim lives in Alliston, Ontario.

In the same collection

Ven Begamudré, *Isaac Brock: Larger Than Life*
Lynne Bowen, *Robert Dunsmuir: Laird of the Mines*
Kate Braid, *Emily Carr: Rebel Artist*
Kathryn Bridge, *Phyllis Munday: Mountaineer*
William Chalmers, *George Mercer Dawson: Geologist, Scientist, Explorer*
Anne Cimon, *Susanna Moodie: Pioneer Author*
Deborah Cowley, *Lucille Teasdale: Doctor of Courage*
Gary Evans, *John Grierson: Trailblazer of Documentary Film*
Julie H. Ferguson, *James Douglas: Father of British Columbia*
Judith Fitzgerald, *Marshall McLuhan: Wise Guy*
lian goodall, *William Lyon Mackenzie King: Dreams and Shadows*
Tom Henighan, *Vilhjalmur Stefansson: Arctic Adventurer*
Stephen Eaton Hume, *Frederick Banting: Hero, Healer, Artist*
Naïm Kattan, *A.M. Klein: Poet and Prophet*
Betty Keller, *Pauline Johnson: First Aboriginal Voice of Canada*
Heather Kirk, *Mazo de la Roche: Rich and Famous Writer*
Vladimir Konieczny, *Glenn Gould: A Musical Force*
Michelle Labrèche-Larouche, *Emma Albani: International Star*
Wayne Larsen, *A.Y. Jackson: A Love for the Land*
Wayne Larsen, *James Wilson Morrice: Painter of Light and Shadow*
Francine Legaré, *Samuel de Champlain: Father of New France*
Margaret Macpherson, *Nellie McClung: Voice for the Voiceless*
Nicholas Maes, *Robertson Davies: Magician of Words*
Dave Margoshes, *Tommy Douglas: Building the New Society*
Marguerite Paulin, *René Lévesque: Charismatic Leader*
Marguerite Paulin, *Maurice Duplessis: Powerbroker, Politician*
Raymond Plante, *Jacques Plante: Behind the Mask*
T.F. Rigelhof, *George Grant: Redefining Canada*
Tom Shardlow, *David Thompson: A Trail by Stars*
Arthur Slade, *John Diefenbaker: An Appointment with Destiny*
Roderick Stewart, *Wilfrid Laurier: A Pledge for Canada*
Sharon Stewart, *Louis Riel: Firebrand*
André Vanasse, *Gabrielle Roy: A Passion for Writing*
John Wilson, *John Franklin: Traveller on Undiscovered Seas*
John Wilson, *Norman Bethune: A Life of Passionate Conviction*
Rachel Wyatt, *Agnes Macphail: Champion of the Underdog*

TECUMSEH

SHOOTING STAR, CROUCHING PANTHER

DUNDURN PRESS
TORONTO

Editor: Allison Hirst   Copy Editor: Cheryl Hawley
Design: Courtney Horner   Printer: Webcom

Library and Archives Canada Cataloguing in Publication

Poling, Jim (Jim R.)
      Tecumseh : shooting star, crouching panther / by Jim Poling Sr.

Includes bibliographical references and index.
ISBN 978-1-55488-414-8

        1. Tecumseh, Shawnee Chief, 1768-1813.   2. Shawnee
Indians--Kings and rulers--Biography.   3. Indians of North
America--Wars--Northwest, Old.   4. Indians of North
America--Wars--1812-1815.   I. Title.

E99.S35T169 2009   974.004'973170092   C2009-900495-X

1   2   3   4   5   13   12   11   10   09

**Conseil des Arts
du Canada**   **Canada Council
for the Arts**

**ONTARIO ARTS COUNCIL
CONSEIL DES ARTS DE L'ONTARIO**

Canadä

We acknowledge the support of the **Canada Council for the Arts** and the **Ontario Arts Council** for our publishing program. We also acknowledge the financial support of the **Government of Canada** through the **Book Publishing Industry Development Program** and **The Association for the Export of Canadian Books**, and the **Government of Ontario** through the **Ontario Book Publishers Tax Credit program**, and the **Ontario Media Development Corporation**.

Care has been taken to trace the ownership of copyright material used in this book. The author and the publisher welcome any information enabling them to rectify any references or credits in subsequent editions.

J. Kirk Howard, President

Printed and bound in Canada.
Printed on recycled paper.

www.dundurn.com

Cover photo: Portrait of Tecumseh from the play *Tecumseh: A Drama* written by Charles Mair, 1886. Artist unknown.

Dundurn Press   Gazelle Book Services Limited   Dundurn Press
3 Church Street, Suite 500   White Cross Mills   2250 Military Road
Toronto, Ontario, Canada   High Town, Lancaster, England   Tonawanda, NY
M5E 1M2   LA1 4XS   U.S.A. 14150

Mixed Sources
Product group from well-managed
forests, and other controlled sources
www.fsc.org Cert no. SW-COC-002358
FSC   © 1996 Forest Stewardship Council

Contents

	Author's Note	7
	Introduction	9
1	A Shooting Star Appears	15
2	Death at Point Pleasant	25
3	Chickamauga Raiders	38
4	Rising Hope, Fallen Timbers	47
5	Descent into Sickness	58
6	Casting Out Witches	69
7	Tippecanoe	85
8	War Comes to Canada	97
9	The Fall of Detroit	105
10	Fort Meigs	117
11	"We Have Met the Enemy …"	129
12	Invasion!	137
13	"The Forlorn Hope"	147
	Epilogue	154
	Chronology of Tecumseh	165
	Sources Consulted	185
	Index	188

Author's Note

Trying to find perfect consistency in North American frontier history, especially where First Nations are involved, is an exercise in frustration. Native people did not have written languages, so spellings of spoken Native words and phrases are so inconsistent as to be distracting. For instance, the word for bear in Ojibwe (*Ojibway, Ojibwa*) can be *maakwaa, muqua, mukwa,* or a number of other combinations of letters that make up the same sounds.

Thus we have *Tecumseh, Tecumseth, Tecumtha, Tecumsay,* and other spellings passed down over the two hundred years since the great chief lived.

There are other inconsistencies that distract: Where was Tecumseh actually born? Where was he at certain times of his life? Exactly how many wives and children did he have? Where is he buried? Military happenings create other inconsistencies.

Each side in a battle or war has its own version of what exactly transpired and how many were killed or wounded.

In reading the history of Tecumseh, variable spellings, lack of precise dates, and inconsistent numbers can be frustrating, but in the end they don't really matter. It's the overall story that counts, the story of a man who stood up for what he believed was right for his people. A man, considered by most white North Americans of the day to be an uneducated savage, who became a symbol of all that is noble in any race.

Scholars continue to frustrate themselves trying to confirm the tiniest details of Tecumseh and his times, while two centuries have further obscured details that were already obscure. Theirs is an important job — to doggedly pursue the latest, best available facts. For the rest of us, what matters most are the main elements of this remarkable life and its impact on Canadian and American history.

Tecumseh lived in much different times, but the story of his life, which is the struggle to protect a vanishing culture, provides lessons for lives lived in any time.

Introduction

Tecumseh's Curse

"Sleep not longer, O Choctaws and Chickasaws, in false security and delusive hopes … Will not the bones of our dead be ploughed up, and their graves turned into ploughed fields?"

— Tecumseh in September 1811, travelling the Mississippi Territory while attempting to unite Indians into a confederacy against U.S. settlement.

Almost fifty years after Tecumseh spoke those words before a council of Choctaws and other Indians, James Dickson, a settler in Southwestern Ontario, ploughed up six skeletons while tending his homestead along the Thames River, east of Chatham. The homestead occupied the battlefield on which

Tecumseh and his British allies were defeated by American invaders on October 5, 1813. Before ploughing, Dickson felled some black walnut trees, which were blazed or carved with animal figures, so the bones were believed to have belonged to Indians, likely Tecumseh and his warriors. Dickson reburied the bones. Some people believed Dickson's discovery fulfilled Tecumseh's prophesy of Indian graves being turned to ploughed fields.

Unearthing the bones was only one unusual event connected to Tecumseh. There are other stories of him predicting his own death, of him foretelling the 1811 New Madrid, Missouri, earthquake that the Creek (Muscogee) Indians believed he caused. The most extraordinary series of events related to Tecumseh is what has become known as Tecumseh's Curse on certain presidents of the United States.

When William Henry Harrison, Tecumseh's nemesis, was sworn into office in March 1841, he caught a pneumonia that killed him thirty-two days after his inauguration. Harrison, one of the most influential figures in the taking of North American Indian land, was elected president in late 1840. He led the army that killed Tecumseh and his dream of a united Indian front against American land grabs west of the Appalachian Mountains.

Twenty years later, in 1860, Abraham Lincoln was elected. He was assassinated before completing his term. James Garfield, elected president in 1880, was also assassinated. William McKinley, re-elected in 1900, was shot and killed. Next was Warren Harding's death in office after his election in 1920.

A pattern was noticed and reported by *Ripley's Believe It Or Not* in the early 1930s. All those presidents who died in office were elected, like Harrison, in a year ending in zero.

From *The Indian Tribes of North America* (1836–44).

The Prophet, Tecumseh's brother. Painting by Charles Bird King.

A story developed that Tecumseh cursed Harrison for destroying Indian life, and that the curse applied to presidents elected in twenty-year intervals after him. Another version had Tenskwatawa the Prophet, Tecumseh's somewhat disturbed brother, laying the curse on Harrison in 1836, the year of Harrison's first attempt to become president, and the year of Tenskwatawa's death.

The Prophet was supposedly having his portrait painted when the presidential election race between Martin Van Buren and Harrison entered the conversation. Tenskwatawa is reported to have said, "Harrison will not win this year to be the great chief. But he may win next time. If he does … he will not finish his term. He will die in office."

"No president has ever died in office," someone challenged.

"But Harrison will die, I tell you," said the Prophet. "And when he dies you will remember my brother Tecumseh's death. You think that I have lost my powers: I who caused the sun to darken and red men to give up firewater. But I tell you, Harrison will die. And after him, every great chief chosen every twenty years thereafter will die. And when each one dies, let everyone remember the death of our people."

After *Ripley's Believe It Or Not* reported the series of unexplainable deaths of presidents elected in years ending with zero, the presidential election of 1940 was watched with interest. Franklin Roosevelt, elected to a third term that year, died in office in 1945. Then Jack Kennedy was elected in 1960, and assassinated before completing his term. There now is an astonishing list of seven U.S. presidents, elected twenty years apart, who have died before completing their respective terms.

Ronald Reagan, elected in 1980, became the first president to escape this unusual string of bad luck, but not completely. He was shot, but his life saved by modern medical technology.

Many people who followed Tecumseh's Curse held their collective breath in the final months of George W. Bush's presidency, which began in 2000. On January 20, 2009, he left the White House, the first U.S. president in almost two hundred years to leave office alive or unharmed after being elected in a year ending with zero.

There is no proof that Tecumseh or his brother pronounced the curse. However, the run of presidential deaths in office is disquieting. *Snopes.com*, a website reporting on urban legends, notes that "Such a string of presidential mortality is too improbable to have occurred naturally...."

Snopes notes that there is no record to support the curse as anything other than an undocumented folktale, but it does take note of some astrological beliefs. Astrologists who analyzed Tecumseh's Curse concluded that the election of the presidents who did not live out their terms coincided with the alignment of Jupiter and Saturn that happens every twenty years. They believe that Reagan was saved by the alignment of these two planets under an air sign, while those who died in office were aligned under an earth sign. Bush was elected in 2000 under the earth sign of Taurus and he survived, so who knows?

One way or another, Tecumseh's Curse, if it ever existed, appears to be done. The same cannot be said for the continuing debate over where Tecumseh's bones rest. For almost two hundred years there has been speculation about where Tecumseh is buried, and attempts to identify his bones. John Richardson, a young soldier-writer who fought beside Tecumseh, made one of the earliest attempts to find Tecumseh's bones, but his 1840 search did not even find the battlefield on which he was captured and Tecumseh died.

There were other attempts, some claiming success in finding the right bones, plus numerous stories that Tecumseh's followers buried him in a creek, or spirited his body away, or that his bones were removed to Walpole Island in the St. Clair River. Over many decades, the controversy over Tecumseh's bones and where they lie has become, at times, a frenzy of ridiculousness.

No one knows for sure where Tecumseh's bones are buried, but most likely they are somewhere in what used to be settler Dickson's field, fulfilling Tecumseh's prophesy that "the bones of our dead be ploughed up, and their graves turned into ploughed fields."

1

A Shooting Star Appears

The March sun warmed and loosened winter's paralysis, stirring new life along every inch of the river's banks. Fern stems poked their pale heads through awakening soil to feel the sunlight. In the forests, little touched by human activity, the trees stretched and felt their saps beginning to flow. Animal life, from bears to the tiniest insects, emerged and set about the business of a new cycle of life.

Nowhere was the activity more evident than among the dozens of tree-bark dwellings near the riverbank. Shawnee children laughed and chased each other around the wigwams in hide-and-seek games while their parents began the chores of the year's most important season. The village's hunter-warriors refurbished tools and weapons, and discussed hunting plans; the women threw themselves into the work of village maintenance and prepared to ready gardens for planting.

Spring meant new life, new beginnings, new adventures, and new workloads.

For a woman called Methoataaskee, the priority task of the spring of 1768 was to deliver the baby she had carried inside her since the previous summer. She lay in a small bark birthing hut near the family lodge, attended by older women. She was twenty-eight and in her fourth pregnancy. The birth came in the evening, just after they had seen a brilliant meteor brighten the darkening sky. Great joy followed the wracking pain of delivery, but the birth created little fanfare. She swaddled the child, a boy, and later strapped him to a *ndiknaagan*, the cradle board that would be with her every work day until he could sit on his own. The birthing done, there were the other children to feed, maple sap to render to syrup and sugar, and corn, squash, and beans to plant.

The new son had his own job: feed, grow, and survive the first delicate months of life. When he abandoned the cradle board some months later, his father, Pukeshinwau, organized his naming feast. The boy took his division or tribal affiliation from his father, a Kispoko Shawnee of the panther clan. Mshibzhii is the celestial panther spirit seen crouching or leaping in the starry skies. The naming was decided by an elder from another clan, who offered tobacco and prayers to the spirits. The name chosen was Tecumtha or Tecumseh, meaning "Shooting Star," and fitting for a life destined to be short, but brilliant.

Tecumseh entered a growing family of some standing. Pukeshinwau, a Kispoko war chief, and Methoataaskee had three sons and a daughter. Cheeseekau had been born seven years earlier, followed by the girl Tecumapease, then Sauawaseekau. The family also included an adopted boy, a white child captured by Pukeshinwau in a raid near Wheeling, West Virginia, a few years earlier. He was born Richard Sparks but the Shawnee renamed him Shawtunte.

The Kispoko village was one of several Shawnee communities along the Scioto River, which started in west-central Ohio, ran 231 miles south through present-day Columbus, and down to Portsmouth, where it joined the mighty Ohio River. The Scioto (*sigh-OH-toe*), an Indian word indicating the presence of many deer, was part of an ancient trail used by the Indians to link their towns and the hunting grounds to the south, in what later became the State of Kentucky.

The Scioto Valley, sitting below the heavily forested Appalachian Foothills, offered the Shawnee the closest thing to paradise. There were open fertile places to plant food crops and the tobacco used for spiritual, medicinal, and cultural purposes. The forests provided life-giving animals including bears, cougars, deer, elk, wild turkeys, wolves, bobcats, and millions of birds — in particular the passenger pigeon, destined for extinction. The river itself was a transport corridor for their elm-bark canoes.

It was a very different land from what we know two hundred years later. The forests were primeval, the rivers and lakes pure, and the only signs of human occupation were footpaths and small habitation clearings. At the time of Tecumseh's birth, roughly 95 percent of the Ohio Territory was covered by mature forest, compared with 30 percent today.

One person's paradise often is another person's envy. The wildlife, good timber, water, and fertile growing areas caught the covetous eyes of the surging population of the Thirteen British Colonies that were spread along the Atlantic Coast, east of the Appalachians. The French, who had settled Canadian lands north and east of the Great Lakes, also felt they had a stake in the Ohio Country, because of their aggressive explorations and fur trading throughout much of the New World.

The interests of both groups were known and watched nervously by the Shawnee and other Indian nations, who already knew the pain of being pushed from their homelands. The powerful Iroquois, expanding their influence and territory in the mid-1600s Beaver Wars, drove the Shawnee from their Ohio River valleys, dispersing some west, some east over the Alleghenies, and others south to the Carolinas, Georgia, Alabama, and as far as Florida. Pukeshinwau was one of these migrants, and it was in the south that he met and married Methoataaskee.

The displaced Shawnees dreamt of regrouping in a traditional homeland south of Lake Erie. One organized reunification occurred in the 1750s with some tribes drifting back to the Ohio Country. Pukeshinwau and Methoataaskee trekked north about 1759, settling along the Scioto River, likely at or near Chillicothe, about 125 miles north of where the Scioto meets the Ohio.

About the same time, the British colonists' interest in the Ohio frontier turned to action. In 1748, some Virginians, including George Washington's half brother Lawrence, formed the Ohio Company, with a plan to get the land west of the Appalachians from King George III of Britain and sell it to settlers for profit. The king granted them two hundred thousand acres of land near what is now the Pennsylvania-Ohio border, even though it wasn't his to give away. It belonged to the North American Indians. The king expected the Company to distribute the land among one hundred families and to build a fort for the settler's safety while they broke the wilderness for farms.

The Virginians knew little about the Ohio Country, so they hired surveyor-frontiersman Christopher Gist to explore the country and to help establish trading relationships with the Indians. Gist liked what he found. On February 17, 1751, he wrote in his journal:

> … rich fine and Level Land, well Timbered with large Walnut, Ash, Sugar Trees, Cherry Trees etc, it is well watered with a great Number of little Streams or Rivulets, and full of beautiful natural Meadows, covered with wild Rye, Blue Grass and clover, and abounds with Turkeys, Deer, and Elks and most sorts of Game particularly Buffaloes, thirty or forty of which are frequently seen feeding in one meadow: In short nothing but Cultivation to make it a most delightful Country — The Ohio and all the large Branches are said to be full of fine Fish …

This was what the Ohio Company wanted to hear. The land could be sold, settled, and cultivated as rich farms. The Company arranged more surveying and initiated land sales with hopes of becoming rich. The colonists saw this as a necessary and natural progression for their new country. Land sales brought important revenues to build the country and enrich many individuals. Little thought was given to the Indian nations who occupied the land. They were considered a lower form of life, indolent and incapable of making the fullest use of the resources that God had provided them.

The Indian view of life could not have been more opposite to that of the colonists. They had everything they needed, and couldn't comprehend why the colonists wanted to accumulate more and more goods that could not be carried into the spirit world. They saw white expansion into their land as an extreme danger, for one simple reason: They lived in balance with nature, small numbers of people living off a limited amount of resources; too many people would tilt the balance, deplete the resources, and everyone would be hungry.

The Indian cycle of living was friendly to the environment. In spring, trees were tapped for syrup, men fished the streams, and women planted small garden plots and gathered herbs and plants from the forest. In summer, crops of berries, ginseng, and other roots and tubers were gathered. Fall brought vegetables from the gardens, and more food from the forests, such as mushrooms. Late fall and winter were the meat hunting seasons. This cycle allowed small groups of people to live off the land without extinguishing its resources. The Indians knew that large groups of settlers knocking down forests to create large farms would upset the cycle.

The French in Canada were alarmed when they heard of the Ohio Company's plans. From their New World along the St. Lawrence, the French had struck out in all directions to explore the wilderness of North America and to establish an ambitious fur trade. They were the first non-Indians into the Ohio Country. The British colonists stayed close to their Atlantic seaboard homes while the French tramped and canoed the West. They believed they had earned the right to the lands below Lake Erie. So they strengthened their claims by dispatching five hundred troops into the region and building forts to enforce their presence.

The French moves sparked the French and Indian War, years of vicious battles between Britain and France for control of North America. It pretty much ended in September 1759, when British general James Wolfe defeated the Marquis de Montcalm on the Plains of Abraham at Quebec City. A year later the British captured Montreal, and in 1763 the two countries signed the Treaty of Paris, giving Britain all of New France, including the Ohio Country, which encompassed the future states of Ohio, Indiana, Illinois, Wisconsin, and Michigan.

The Shawnee supported the French in the war because the French understood the Indians better than most Europeans, and generally treated them as allies, rather than pawns. The Shawnee feared that if the British defeated the French, settlers from the Thirteen Colonies would pour over the Appalachians into the Ohio Country and destroy the Indian way of life. Much to their surprise, King George III had the same fears. In October 1763, Britain passed a Royal Proclamation closing all Indian territories west of the Appalachians to the colonists. It also placed all Indians under the protection of the king.

George III and his advisers were not simply being nice to the Indians. The British king wanted to improve the fur trade in North America and he needed the Indians for that. Also, he wanted his colonists, showing signs of rebellion against him, corralled along the Atlantic seaboard where they could be better regulated. The Ohio Company, its deal with King George superseded, was now without lands to sell and was forced out of business. This appeared to be good fortune for the Shawnee and other Indian nations in the Ohio Country. The threat of a white invasion from the east was suspended, and 1768, the year of Tecumseh's birth, promised a time of calm with hope for a peaceful future.

Without war, Shawnee life was reasonably carefree. The land, as long as it remained relatively unpopulated, provided adequate food and shelter. Life was a constant struggle against nature, but the Indians had centuries of experience and the Shawnee were intelligent and industrious. Women and girls nurtured gardens, collected food, stoked fires, made clothes, and tended to the maintenance of the bark or hide wigwams. Men gambled, smoked, talked, and tended to weapons and tools — and made war. In autumn, families dispersed, travelling to winter hunting grounds where the men sought out the animals needed for food, clothing, tools, and trade.

The child Tecumseh was as free as the animals his elders pursued. His life was outside — running, swimming, learning to build tools and weapons, such as the bow and arrow. He and his pals practised hunting and played war games. Decades later, Tecumseh's war play was described by Stephen Ruddell, a white youth captured by the Shawnee:

> During his boyhood he used to place himself at the head of the youngsters and divide them … he would make them fight sham battles in which he always distinguished himself by his activity, strength, and skill.

Ruddell was another white boy who grew up with the Shawnee after they snatched him during a raid on Ruddell's Station, a small settlement in Kentucky. He and Tecumseh became blood brothers, sharing war games, and later hunting expeditions and real war.

The war games were important for Shawnee boys because their destiny was not to live in peace. The frontier was always alive with war talk, if only squabbles between tribes or small skirmishes between the Indians and intruders on their territory.

King George's proclamation protecting the Ohio Country and its Indians did not last long. The year Tecumseh was born, the Iroquois Six Nations Confederacy, which had claimed the Ohio Country since the 1600s, sold part of it to the colonists for ten thousand pounds. Other tribes protested that the land belonged to all Indians and it was not up to the Iroquois alone to sell it. Not long after the sale, the Shawnee watched a new procession of surveyors and settlers from the Thirteen Colonies float down the Ohio River to open new settlements. The colonists, who had started to call themselves Patriots or Americans, ignored the King's proclamation. This was no big deal for them because they no longer tolerated King George and his laws from abroad. Differences between the new Americans and the British set off the American Revolution, which began as Tecumseh approached the age of reason.

The Revolution impacted all tribes south of Lake Erie, directly and dramatically. The breakaway colonists were expansionists who wanted the Indian lands west of the Appalachians. The British, although they had broken promises before, offered some hope of protection against this expansion if they could put down the American revolt. They needed allies against the upstart Americans, so they gave the Indians guns and supplies, and while reminding them of King George's promised protection, incited them into raids on American settlements.

In the summer of 1774, Tecumseh's sixth year, the Shawnee boy's life and the future of his people was decided. Colonists in Virginia, taking control of the new lands given up by the Iroquois, decided to crush any Indian resistance, which included the Shawnee. The Indians called the Virginians "Long Knives" or "Big Knives," because of the long swords carried by colonial military officers, and later the name was applied to all Americans. The Long Knives marched on the Ohio Country, determined to destroy the Shawnee villages along the Scioto.

The leaves were changing colour when Pukeshinwau received a messenger delivering a red tomahawk, the call to war chiefs to gather for war. Young Tecumseh, the drums pounding in his ears, watched his father's warriors strip to breechcloths and prepare their weapons. They painted their faces and shaved their heads to scalp locks. They drank vegetable potions, fasted, and called on the spirits for success in war.

One can imagine the emotions of a six-year-old boy standing with his mother and siblings as the war party prepared to leave. The whoops of warriors and the neighing of excited horses rolling through the autumn air already filled with dust, the smell of horse flesh, tension, and determination. He must have been overcome with envy and pride as his older brother Cheeseekau, just thirteen, took his place in the war party beside his father.

Tecumseh and his family watched the war party disappear in the distance, Methoataaskee with a large belly that told of another child to come in winter. Tecumseh ached for the day that he would join them on the trail to war. He could not know, however, that his own path to war would be part of a desperate struggle to save his people. Neither did he know that he would never see his father again.

2

Death at Point Pleasant

Shawnee Chief Hokoleskwa, known in English as Cornstalk, preferred peace, but in the autumn of 1774 he had little choice but to fight. Long Knives from Virginia marched into a Mingo Indian village on the Ohio River, near today's Pennsylvania-Ohio border, and massacred eleven people, including the headman's mother and sister. The Mingos, a mixed tribe of mainly Iroquois, were generally peaceful and were outraged. They found support among the Shawnee, who were seeking revenge for the deaths of some tribesmen in separate incidents.

Mingos and Shawnee attacked white settlements in Pennsylvania to even the score. They killed thirteen settlers and handed Lord Dunmore, the British governor of Virginia, an excuse to settle the growing Indian problem. Dunmore retaliated against two Shawnee villages near the current West

Virginia border, then assembled two armies to march on the Indian towns along the Scioto.

Cornstalk wanted to avoid war but it was coming at him, so he sent the red tomahawk to Shawnee chiefs throughout the central Ohio Territory. The red tomahawk put Pukeshinwau and his warriors on the war trail south to meet Cornstalk and the main assembly of warriors.

Cornstalk planned to take the offensive. He had three to five hundred warriors prepared to hit the Virginia army near where the Kanawha River meets the Ohio in southern Ohio. Early in the morning of October 10, 1774, Cornstalk, Pukeshinwau, and their warriors crossed the Ohio River and met the Long Knives at Point Pleasant. The fighting was severe, much of it hand-to-hand, and raged until near nightfall. Cornstalk was heard shouting above the battle clamour for his warriors to "be strong" and carry the fight. The Shawnee were hugely outnumbered, however, and by day's end retreated back across the river.

The Shawnee lost the battle, but the Virginians paid heavily, with seventy-five dead and 150 wounded. Perhaps forty Shawnee were dead, but no count was available because the Indians threw their dead into the Ohio to prevent the Long Knives from scalping and mutilating them. Mutilating enemy corpses was a common feature of North American frontier warfare. All sides — Indians, British, French, and Americans — did it. The whites scalped to terrorize the Indians and play on their superstitions about scalp locks containing spiritual power. They also encouraged their people, and Indians allied to them, to take enemy scalps in return for cash bounties. It was a savage practice that grew throughout the 1700s because of the use of official bounties.

The Indians, before bounties were offered, sometimes kept scalps as trophies, hanging them from poles or along the gunwales of canoes. The practice was witnessed by Thomas Gist, the son of the Ohio Country surveyor, after he was held prisoner by a group of Indians in the Ohio Country:

> The men began to scrape the flesh and blood from the scalps, and dry them by the fire, after which they dressed them with feathers and painted them, then tied them on white, red, and black poles.

In Tecumseh's time, scalping was done by shoving the victim, dead or alive, face first into the ground, pushing a foot or knee between the shoulders, yanking the head back by the hair, then making a crescent slice along the forehead and ripping the scalp back.

A scalping was described by John Richardson, the teenager who served with the British and Tecumseh, and who later became a famous Canadian writer. He wrote of an Indian chief at the 1813 Battle of the Thames throwing a tomahawk at a Kentuckian's head, then:

> Laying down his rifle, he drew forth his knife, and after having removed the hatchet from the brain, proceeded to make a circular incision throughout the scalp. This done, he grasped the bloody instrument between his teeth, and placing his knees on the back of his victim, while at the same time he fastened his fingers in the hair, the scalp was torn off without much apparent difficulty and thrust, still bleeding, into his bosom. The warrior then arose, and having

wiped his knife on the clothes of the unhappy man, returned it to its sheath, grasping at the same time the arms he had abandoned, and hastening to rejoin his comrades. All this was the work of a few minutes.

Scalping was only one indignity committed on the battlefield. The Virginians and Kentuckians were well known for stripping skin from Indians bodies, using it for razor strops and other household accessories. Some of most heroic frontier battlefield stories are about Indians recovering dead comrades to save their bodies from mutilation. The Indians were adept at recovering their dead and secretly burying them or dropping them into streams, a practice that became an interesting issue with the death of Tecumseh years later.

One of the Shawnee dead at Point Pleasant was Pukeshinwau. His young son Cheeseekau was at his side when he died. The story of the death was related throughout the Shawnee community and Stephen Ruddell later recounted what he had been told:

> At his dying moment he called to him his oldest son, a youth of twelve or thirteen years … and strongly enjoined on him to preserve unsullied the dignity and honour of his family; and directed him in future to lead forth to battle his younger brothers.

Cheeseekau followed a sorrowful trail home with the surviving Shawnee and set to work looking after his younger brothers, especially Tecumseh, instructing them in the arts of living and war. By winter's end he had two more brothers to train; Methoataaskee had given birth to triplets, one of whom died. One of the surviving boys, Lalawéthika, was destined to play a huge role in helping Tecumseh make history.

Pukeshinwau was not the only Tecumseh family member lost in the Point Pleasant battle. The defeat forced the Shawnee into a peace treaty in which they agreed to give up their white captives. Shawtunte, now about fourteen, was sought by his parents who had heard about the treaty. They found him but he didn't recognize them, nor could he speak English. His mother identified him by a birthmark. He returned home with his parents, and later became a scout for the new United States Army. He eventually attained the rank of colonel.

Tecumseh's boyhood was filled with war. The Americans, fighting for complete independence from Britain, worried about the British coming at them from the back door — the northwest Indian country south and west of Lake Erie. Out there the Shawnee were supporting the British in the hopes that the Americans would be beaten, and defeat would end the flow of American settlers and militias crossing into their lands from Pennsylvania, Virginia, and Kentucky. The Shawnee knew that more settlers meant more farms, less forest, and diminished game, which in turn meant more reliance on trade goods and white lifestyles. With British help they intended to push the Americans back across the mountains.

The Indians were the ones who got pushed, however. They were pushed from eastern Ohio, from the Scioto and the Mad rivers, and later from the Great and Little Miami rivers in western Ohio into present-day Indiana. Eventually they were pushed completely out of the lives they had known for hundreds of years before people first arrived from Europe.

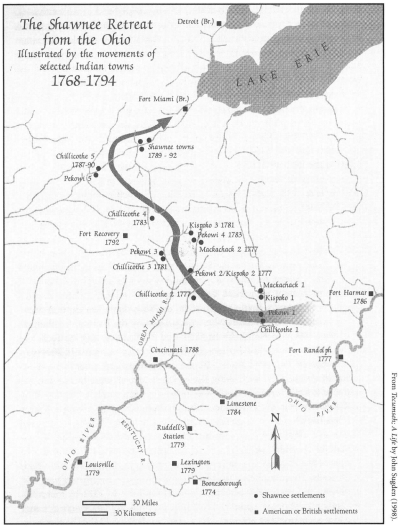

The Shawnee Retreat from the Ohio, 1768–94.

In 1777, the wars forced the Shawnee to abandon much of their Scioto River homeland. They moved west to be less open to American attacks. Methoataaskee moved her family to the northwest bank of Mad River, just west of present-day Springfield, Ohio. It was safer and an excellent playground for the Shawnee children. The new village stood on a hill overlooking the river, with panoramic views of forests interspersed with small prairies. There were limestone cliffs behind the village, which the children climbed and explored, and a small swamp in which they developed hunting skills.

The Mad River area offered relative safety and serenity. Tecumseh and his siblings grew under the direction of Methoataaskee, until she decided to move south to Cherokee country, perhaps because she had taken another husband. The raising of Tecumseh and the younger children fell to the oldest brother, Cheeseekau, and older sister, Tecumapease.

The serenity of the Mad River was short-lived. In the summer of 1780, the western Ohio countryside was engulfed in the flames of war. The British assembled a large war group of soldiers and Indians along the Mad River, and marched south to attack settlements in Kentucky. They grabbed 350 prisoners, including young Stephen Ruddell, who met Tecumseh in one of the Indian encampments. Here they began their lifelong friendship.

The raid stunned the Kentuckians. They struck back hard with forces led by George Rogers Clark, who became known as a famous Indian fighter. They raided Shawnee villages, killing, capturing, and putting wigwams and fields into flame. On August 8, they arrived at Tecumseh's village on the Mad River. Women and children were sent up to the bluffs for protection, while the warriors positioned themselves for battle. Clark advanced with a six-pound cannon, and after two days the Shawnee villages were destroyed. Tecumseh and his family, then war refugees, fled with other Shawnee farther up the Mad River, as far as the Little Miami River.

That was a turning point in the history of wars against Indians. The Americans realized that killing Indian warriors only made them more determined. Younger warriors were pushed forward to replace the missing, and more white captives, like young Ruddell, were taken to fill holes in the ranks. It was more effective to burn homes and crops because warriors who were forced to constantly find food and shelter for their starving people had little time for war.

The raids along the Mad River resulted in small numbers of Shawnee deaths, but the loss of homes and ripening crops was devastating. Morale was further smashed by the savagery of the Kentuckians, who plundered graves for scalps. The hungry Shawnee found themselves begging the British for food. They continued to fight, but the future of all Indians in the Ohio Country was becoming clear; the Americans were a force capable of conquering the Northwest.

The Revolutionary War ended in 1783, with Britain ceding all lands south of the Great Lakes and east of the Mississippi River to the new American nation. The war's end promised only a temporary peace for the Ohio Country Indians, who continued to worry about the coming of more American settlers. The British had signed away the Northwest Indian Territory with no regard for native rights, but they had not withdrawn their protection completely. They kept some forts such as Niagara, Detroit, and Michilimackinac for thirteen years after the war because they said the Americans were not living up to all the conditions of the 1783 peace treaty.

Living between the British and the Americans was like being caught in a vice. The Indians compared the two nations to the two separate blades on a pair of scissors. John Heckewelder, a longtime Moravian missionary on the frontier, described this Indian analogy in his book about Indian customs and culture:

> I have heard them, for instance, compare the English and American nations to a pair of scissors, an instrument composed of two sharp edged knives exactly alike, working against each other for the same purpose, that of cutting. By the construction of this instrument, they said, it would appear as if in shutting, these two sharp knives would strike each together and destroy each other's sharp edges; but no such thing: they only cut what comes between them. And thus the English and Americans do when they go to war against one another. It is not each other they want to destroy, but us, poor Indians, that are between them. By this means they get our land, and, when that is obtained, the scissors are closed again, and laid by for further use.

Tecumseh entered his formative teenage years and his older siblings directed him into manhood. Cheeseekau gave him the critical knowledge of how to live off the land, hunt, and trap and how to become successful on the war trails. Tecumapease instilled in him the important human traits of honour, compassion, and doing what was right.

Teenage years are years of confusion, but they must have been especially confusing for the teenagers of Tecumseh's time. They knew little peace. Blood and flames were constants in their lives. They watched the old ways of Indian life disappear, as they struggled against a wave of newcomers bringing disease, destructive customs, and a lust for land that could not be satisfied.

In these circumstances, Tecumseh might have been expected to grow up negative, embittered, and savagely vengeful. History shows, however, that he turned out generous, intelligent, and good natured. He was among the most fearsome warriors in battle, adept at killing with war club, bow and arrow, scalping knife, or musket, but able to demonstrate a compassion not expected for the times.

Cheeseekau, as his elder brother, guided him on his vision quest, a rite of passage for most North American Indian boys and girls. They were sent out onto the land and, through meditation and deprivation, were to receive power from their spirits. They were expected to see visions of one or more spirits in the form of an animal, bird, or natural force, such as a storm. These visions came from the Master of Life, Waashaa Monetoo to the Shawnee.

Stephen Ruddell once described Cheeseekau's influence on young Tecumseh:

> [H]e took upon himself the education of his brothers and used every means to instill into the mind of Tecumtheth correct, manly and honourable principles, leading him forth himself to battle and instructing him in warfare. He taught him to look with contempt upon everything that was mean …

Ruddell called Tecumseh a born leader and an exceptionally good hunter:

He was a great hunter and what was remarkable [was that] he would never if he could avoid it hunt in parties where women were. He was free hearted and generous to excess — always ready to relieve the wants of others. Whenever he returned from a hunting expedition he would harangue his companions, and made use of all his eloquence to instill into their minds honourable and humane sentiments.

Tecumseh and Ruddell often hunted together as boys. One day they heard hunters chasing buffalo with dogs. They climbed into the trees under which the buffalo would pass. Ruddell dropped one of the running beasts with a single-shot musket. Tecumseh fired arrow after arrow into the passing animals and dropped sixteen, a number likely exaggerated by the telling.

Tecumseh grew out of his teen years as a well-built and handsome man. He stood five feet, ten inches tall, and was athletic. Ruddell later described him as an extremely active person and quite strong. There is no record of his first battles, but he was certain to have been riding with Cheeseekau, then a warrior of some note, on hunting parties and skirmishes in his early to mid-teens. A story is told of the Shawnee fighting Kentucky militia along the Mad River. Tecumseh the teenager was said to have become afraid and fled while Cheeseekau, wounded, continued the fight.

It is an unlikely story considering Indian boys were taught from birth to hunt and fight, and when they reached their teens they were obsessed with the thoughts of their first battles. Warrior is a profession among the Indians. Some boys were raised to become medicine men, others civil leaders, while the job of the warrior-hunter was to fight and kill and be killed. Also, the savagery of the times in which the Shawnee were most often engulfed in war made it unlikely that an Indian boy was afraid of anything.

In 1786–87, Tecumseh turned eighteen and two things occurred to ensure that the Shawnee would have many more battles against the Long Knives. The new U.S. Congress, desperate for revenue and hungry for more settlement, annexed the lands west of the Appalachians, which became known as the Northwest Territory. This guaranteed a new migration of settlers from the east, something the Shawnee and some other tribes would not tolerate. However, land sales faltered because prospective settlers were afraid to live in a war zone.

That autumn, a Long Knives' militia crossed the Ohio near Limestone and hit a village that was only partially occupied because many people had moved off to winter hunting grounds. Some of the villagers raised an American flag in a vain attempt to stop the attack. The Long Knives killed some villagers then rounded up the rest as prisoners. One prisoner was the elderly chief called Moluntha, who was interrogated by an American colonel about an earlier battle in which the Kentuckians had suffered a humiliating defeat. The colonel did not like the answers he received and hit the old chief with the flat side of a tomahawk, knocking him to the ground. As the old man struggled to get up, the colonel sunk the tomahawk into his skull, then scalped him.

More settlement, and more atrocities like the killing of a defenceless elder, enraged the Shawnee. They rampaged through what is now western Pennsylvania, West Virginia, eastern Ohio, and north Kentucky. One of their favourite spots was along the Ohio River, because the transportation artery floated hundreds of settlers downriver toward new homes and new lives in Kentucky. Tecumseh was a regular among the warriors who attacked settlers' flatboats, rich targets loaded with livestock and household possessions. The Indians launched bark canoes or simply waited at narrow spots in the river to make interceptions. Sometimes they stood white captives on the shore as decoys to lure boats into landing.

The large flatboats, some nearly one hundred feet in length, were propelled and steered by long oars, requiring four to six men as crew. When they had to man the oars in difficult situations, the men could not fight back. That's when the Indians poured musket balls and arrows at them.

Tecumseh was among a band of Indians that attacked a large flatboat being brought downriver by traders. The Shawnee captured the boat and killed all the people aboard, except one. This man was taken prisoner and later burned alive. Tecumseh watched the burning, but was young, with no status to interfere. The burning scene seared his memory. He told other warriors of his disgust of torture and promised himself that he would prevent such brutality in future.

Dislike of needless cruelty became a Tecumseh characteristic. He believed it was wrong to murder helpless captives and was not afraid to tell others.

"He was always averse to taking prisoners in his warfare," Ruddell wrote later in life. "But when prisoners fell into his hands he always treated them with as much humanity as if they had been in the hands of civilized people — no burning — no torturing. He never tolerated the practice of killing women and children."

3

Chickamauga Raiders

The Shawnee of Tecumseh's time were wanderers. Probably no other North American Indian nation split so often and moved so much. Some of their movements were dictated by politics and war, like when the Iroquois pushed them from the Ohio Country valleys in the 1600s. This displacement saw them mingle with other nations; the Cherokee and Seminoles, among others.

Aside from that, they enjoyed moving about. They were a congenial people who liked visiting and socializing. They were well accepted by other Indian nations and adept at good relations and the art of diplomacy. They were Algonquian speakers, meaning they spoke a dialect of one of North America's most widespread Indian tongues, and the language facilitated movements among others.

Their style of living also made moving about easier. Their bark houses were quickly rebuilt wherever forests existed. Thin but sturdy poles lashed together made a house framework to which they attached large pieces of bark. When bark was not available, or when time was an issue, animal skins were fitted over the frame.

As a youth, Tecumseh was driven from place to place on the Ohio frontier by the advancement of the whites. As he grew to adulthood he travelled with Cheeseekau for hunting and for raids aimed at stopping the encroachment of settlements. Later he would travel even more extensively — by horse, canoe, and on foot — in his efforts to organize Indians into a confederacy to stop the settlers.

Tecumseh was twenty when Cheeseekau organized a major move. He planned to relocate to Spanish-held territory in Missouri. Many of the Shawnee were tired of the settlers' encroachments and the constant wars. At this time, North America was divided up between the British, who had Canada, the Spanish, who had much of the territory west of the Mississippi, and the Americans, who were expanding across the Appalachians. They were all rivals and drew the Indians into warfare to further their own purposes.

The Shawnee brothers and their followers travelled at the invitation of an enterprising fellow named Louis Lorimier, a Montrealer who traded south of Lake Erie. Lorimier spoke several Indian languages, had a Shawnee-French wife, and had helped the Indians fight American settlement on the Ohio frontier. All that made him a rogue in American eyes, and he fled the American advancement on the Ohio Country for Spanish Territory west of the Mississippi River. He opened a new trading business at Ste. Genevieve (Missouri) then hatched a plan to colonize the area with Shawnee and Delaware Indians. The Spanish liked his idea because they wanted to build their presence in the West to help ward off the hostile Osage Indians and the new United States of America.

Cheeseekau and Tecumseh were among two hundred Shawnee and Delawares who left the Ohio frontier for Missouri in the summer and fall of 1788. A hunting accident delayed the trip. Tecumseh was chasing buffalo when he was thrown from his horse and broke his thigh bone. He could not travel, so the group set up a winter camp. The leg was still not fully healed when spring arrived, but Cheeseekau said they could wait no longer and suggested that Tecumseh stay behind with a few warriors until he was fit to travel. Tecumseh refused and resumed the Missouri trek, using crutches when he had to walk. The injury left him with a limp and one leg bowed and shorter than the other.

Lorimier had land for them when they arrived, but they were not the only newcomers. The Spanish had made a deal with a former United States Indian Agent to bring in American settlers who were building New Madrid on the banks of Mississippi. He warned the Americans not to interfere with the Indians, but it wasn't long before trouble started. Some Americans passing through the area shot at Delaware and Cherokee hunters and stole their furs. The Indians were outraged and talked of burning New Madrid in retaliation, but that cooled. Cheeseekau saw, however, that sharing the territory with Americans was not going to work. Soon after arriving, his group left, crossed the Mississippi, and headed south to the Tennessee River Territory to join the Chickamauga War against American settlement.

The Chickamauga War had raged for twelve years before Cheeseekau and Tecumseh arrived. The worst of it had begun in 1776, at the beginning of the American Revolution. Tribes from north of the Ohio River, encouraged and supported by the British, had urged Cherokee tribes to join in the war against the Americans. The Cherokee raided white settlements east of the Appalachians, but succumbed to the white man's musket balls, diseases, and land grabs. The British then offered guns, ammunition, money for scalps, and a powerful alliance to launch new efforts against the breakaway colonists.

Most of the Cherokees declined and remained neutral. Some, led by the fierce fighter Tsi'-yu-gunsi-ni, or Dragging Canoe, attacked American settlements, killing, scalping, and taking captives. The Americans retaliated, attacking thirty Cherokee villages and destroying houses and crops. The main body of Cherokees, most of whom had not fought, signed "peace" treaties in 1777, ceding five million acres of land to the Americans.

Dragging Canoe refused to recognize the treaties and took his rebels to Chickamauga Creek, which flowed into the Tennessee River at present-day Chattanooga. They built village strongholds in the forested mountains overlooking the Tennessee, and raided white settlements and the boats bringing even more settlers downriver. They became known as Chickamaugas to distinguish them from the Cherokees who signed the treaties. They were not just Cherokees, but Creeks, Shawnees, and other Indians, plus rebel whites and African Americans who were opposed to the settlement of the Tennessee frontier.

Cheeseekau and Tecumseh join the Chickamaugas because they could not find a more fierce or powerful ally in the struggle against settlement. They were all brothers in a family of oppressed people. The Chickamauga Cherokees had often visited Shawnee villages in Ohio, promoting the fight against the Americans. And the Shawnee were no strangers to the wild Tennessee frontier. They had lived on the Cumberland River in northern Tennessee during the late 1600s and early 1700s, until they were displaced by the Chickasaws, who had been powerful enough at the time to enforce hunting rights over the wildlife rich Tennessee and Kentucky wilderness.

The brothers and their warriors arrived among the Chickamaugas in late 1789, or early 1790, and immediately joined raiding parties attacking settlements and boats coming down the Tennessee River. It was a repeat of the Ohio River days: hit and run raids to discourage settlement.

One raid was against a barge being brought upriver. It was manned by sixteen American soldiers commanded by a major. The Indians approached the barge and Cheeseekau talked to the major, feigning friendship. Later, when the soldiers put down their arms to man the oars, the Indians opened fire on them. More than half of the Americans were killed or wounded and their mission, which the Indians believed was to build a fort in the area, was aborted.

In another attack the Shawnees poured musket fire into a passing barge and when it drifted ashore they found thirty-two men dead or wounded.

Their raids were effective. They slowed the rate of settlement, forcing some land development companies to delay or even abandon plans for settlements. Cheeseekau and others hit hard at Cumberland River settlements near Nashville, spreading panic among the settlers. For a while, the Chickamaugas believed that the war against settlement might be won.

On June 26, 1792, Cheeseekau and others hit a settlement called Ziegler's Station near where Nashville now stands. Twenty-one people gathered in a blockhouse for safety, but the warriors set fire to vacant buildings and watched the flames spread to the blockhouse. When the fire became intense, a young man opened the door and was shot in the chest as he ushered out his wife and six children. Other men bolted for freedom. Some of them escaped, but others were killed. Jacob Ziegler was burned to death inside his house.

Women and children captives were marched through the forest, the children in bare feet. At one point, the Indians stopped and made little moccasins for them, an incredible contrast to the savagery of the raid. One man in a pursuing posse commented: "At the next muddy spot, we saw little footprints of moccasins. There was that much kindness in them (the Indians)."

Cheeseekau released three children a few weeks later, in return for fifty-eight dollars each. The taking of captives was an important part of Indian warfare. Captives were useful as fighters or slaves, or as currency in trade for almost anything.

Tecumseh is not named anywhere as being part of that raiding party, but that does not mean he was not there. He had gone north to Ohio the year before, when tribes there issued a call for help in a major offensive expected from the Long Knives. However, he certainly was among the Chickamaugas about three months after the Ziegler's Station raid, and was part of an attack that would bring more personal tragedy.

In September 1792, war chiefs gathered at Lookout Mountain at Chattanooga to plot more campaigns against the settlers. There were heated arguments about whether the Americans were too powerful to defeat, and whether it was better to stop fighting and accept their gifts. Cheeseekau was enraged. He stepped forward among the chiefs, raised his hands, and declared:

"With these hands I have killed three hundred, and I will kill three hundred more, drink my fill of blood, and sit down and be happy."

The chiefs agreed. There would be a new campaign of killing and destruction along the Tennessee and Cumberland rivers — one to shock the whites into abandoning their settlements.

Buchanan's Station was four miles south of Nashville; a typical frontier settlement. Its few log cabins were protected by a log palisade and blockhouse occupying a rise on Mill Creek, near where it flowed into the Cumberland. Late on the night of September 30, Cheeseekau and roughly thirty Shawnee slipped through the shadows created by a bright and full moon, advancing silently on the settlement. A shadow flickered and alarmed the livestock, which grew restless and set the dogs to barking. Two sentries in the blockhouse peered out their port holes and saw the Indians advancing. They fired shots and the Indians began pouring shots into the blockhouse port holes.

There are differing stories about what happened that night. One is that the sentries' first shot struck Cheeseekau in the centre of the forehead, killing him instantly. The other is that the Indians tried for an hour to take the station and Cheeseekau was trying to set fire to the blockhouse when he was hit by a musket ball. As he died, he is said to have told the warriors, including Tecumseh, that he was happy to die in battle rather than in a wigwam like an old woman.

Tecumseh took his brother's body from the scene and gave him a traditional Shawnee burial. Death was constant in the warrior's life, but the death of Cheeseekau was especially bitter for his younger brother. Cheeseekau taught him to be a skilled and respected hunter and warrior. He had been the father they had lost in another battle against the settlers many years before.

Tecumseh not only grieved for his brother, he grieved for all his people and the apparently impossible mission of dislodging the Americans from the Indian homelands. It must have been apparent that not only were the Indians losing battles, they were losing the overall war to keep their way of life and their independence.

Tecumseh decided to return to Ohio, but Shawnee custom demanded he avenge Cheeseekau's death. The days following the Buchanan's Station fiasco saw raids in the Nashville area: individual cabins attacked and burned, settlers killed, soldiers killed in a blockhouse. The Indians did not keep records so it is not known which raids were the work of Tecumseh.

A few weeks later, on Cumberland Mountain in Central Tennessee, there came evidence of Tecumseh's revenge: Indians had waited in ambush near Walton Trace, where a creek crossed the forest path. Captain Samuel Handley and his forty-two militiamen had been fording the creek with their horses when musket fire filled the air. Eight militiamen fell dead while most of the others fled down the trail toward Knoxville.

Captain Handley was taken alive. The Indians gave him rough treatment, making him run the gauntlet and preparing him for burning one or more times. The gauntlet was an Indian blood sport in which captives were forced to run between two lines of warriors, and sometimes women, holding sticks, clubs, and tomahawks. The idea was to see if the captive had the skills and courage to run through the lines while fending off blows.

Handley survived the gauntlet and was saved from burning by the intercession of a chief. Witnesses said the chief was Shawnee, was visiting in the south, and had a mother living with the Cherokee. Tecumseh's mother Methoataaskee was believed to have left the Shawnee to live with the Cherokee in the south, a few years after her husband's death at Point Pleasant. Historians say the evidence points to Tecumseh having led the attack and sparing Handley, who was later released. During his captivity, Handley suffered a fever that caused his hair to fall out. It grew back pure white.

Tecumseh returned to Ohio, no longer the teenager travelling in the moccasin tracks of his big brother. He was his own man, fully grown, battle hardened, and a leader. He demonstrated his leadership soon after crossing the Ohio River near the mouth of the Scioto in December 1792. His small party, ten or so braves, stopped to hunt near Big Rock in southern Ohio. One morning the men were at their campfire, smoking and talking, when shots rang out. Tecumseh organized his men in returning fierce fire, and forced the attackers to retreat. He killed one and might have killed more had he not broken the trigger on his musket. The attackers were triple the number of the Shawnee, who suffered only two wounded, while the Americans were pushed away with two dead.

The fight was another successful adventure that added to Tecumseh's growing reputation as a leader of warriors. Strong leadership was what the Indians would need for future major battles to stop the runaway flow of settlers into the Northwest Territory.

4

Rising Hope, Fallen Timbers

Tecumseh returned home to find many Indian villages of the Northwest jubilant and full of hope for holding back the tide of American settlement. While he fought in the south, pockets of Northwest Indians from different nations and tribes joined together to inflict much pain on the American settlers, their militias, and the new U.S. Army. The sting was felt personally by President George Washington who, in 1790, ordered a major offensive to end the Indian uprisings that were slowing settlement on both sides of the Ohio River.

The new offensive was a disaster. Late in 1790, General Josiah Harmar was at the head of almost fifteen hundred troops assembled near what is now the Ohio-Indiana border. He decided to commit only part of his force — four hundred troops under Colonel John Hardin — to attack eleven hundred warriors. The Indians mauled Hardin's force, handing him more than two hundred casualties and forcing him into a humiliating retreat. The Indians also mauled another part of Harmar's force, sending what was left of the army on a bloody trail back to Fort Washington, now Cincinnati.

President Washington was upset and ordered the governor of the Northwest Territory, Arthur St. Clair, to take another large force and end the Indian uprisings. He warned the fifty-five-year-old St. Clair to beware of a surprise attack.

On November 4, 1791, a large part of General St. Clair's army of fourteen hundred men slumbered peacefully along the Wabash River. It was a bitterly cold dawn, and the soldiers and militia stacked their rifles while they prepared a morning meal. Shouts, followed by shots, sent the camp into panic as one thousand Indians, led by Blue Jacket and Miami Chief Little Turtle, overran the Americans.

One officer, Major Ebenezer Denny wrote in his journal:

> The savages seemed not to fear anything we could do. They could skip out of reach of bayonet and return, as they pleased. The ground was literally covered with the dead ... It appeared as if the officers had been singled out, as a very great proportion fell. The men being thus left with few officers, became fearful, despaired of success, gave up the fight.

More than six hundred Americans — regulars, militia, and camp followers, including women, died that cold morning. The Indians stuffed soil into the mouths of some dead to mock their lust for land. It made Custer's Last Stand, in which 263 soldiers died later in 1876, look like a disrupted picnic.

Washington demanded that St. Clair resign his army commission and raged:

> To suffer that army to be cut to pieces, hacked, butchered, tomahawked by surprise — the very thing I guarded him against — O God! O God! … How can he answer to his country!

Those victories buoyed the Indian movement. The Indians talked of driving the Americans back across the Ohio River and the Appalachians, and making the Northwest Territory truly theirs again. The Battle of the Wabash reinforced Tecumseh's belief that only a strong confederacy of Indian nations could defeat the Long Knives. St. Clair's army had been humbled by a united force of Shawnee, Miamis, Delawares, Ojibwe, Ottawas, Potawatomis, Wyandots, Cherokees, and even some Seneca and Cayugas of the Iroquois nations.

Building new battle confederacies was not a new idea. Indians had tried uniting against white rule in the past, as recently as the early 1760s in what became known as Pontiac's Rebellion.

Pontiac's uprising had followed the 1763 Treaty of Paris, which ended French rule and, in turn, brought on less happy times for the Indians of the Northwest. The British who replaced the French were haughty and treated the Indians with much less respect, even disdain. New British policies restricted the amount of guns, ammunition, foodstuffs, and other supplies that the Indians received. Many Indians felt this was a British tactic to disarm them and take their land for settlement.

Pontiac, a chief of the Ottawas, summed up the Indian feelings at a war council near Fort Detroit:

It is important for us, my brothers, that we exterminate from our lands this nation which seeks only to destroy us. You see as well as I do that we can no longer supply our needs, as we have done from our brothers, the French. The English sell us goods twice as dear as the French do, and their goods do not last. Scarcely have we bought a blanket or something else to cover ourselves with before we must think of getting another; and when we wish to set out for our winter camp they do not want to give us any credit as our brothers the French do.

When I go to see the English commander and say to him that some of our comrades are dead, instead of bewailing their death, as our French brothers do, he laughs at me and at you. If I ask for anything for our sick, he refuses with the reply that he has no use for us. From all this you can well see that they are seeking our ruin. Therefore, my brothers, we must all swear their destruction and wait no longer. Nothing prevents us: They are few in numbers, and we can accomplish it.

Indian resentment grew until Pontiac organized a confederacy and attacked Fort Detroit, in May 1763. The attack turned into a siege but the fort was not taken. During the following months, however, Pontiac's confederacy captured eight British forts, killing or capturing as many as two thousand soldiers and settlers, and forcing several thousand settlers to flee their homesteads. Some historians report that the British distributed goods infected with smallpox to eliminate the Indians.

By 1764, the British colonies were so panicked by constant Indian attacks that two serious military expeditions were sent into the Ohio Country to subdue the Indians. Finally, in 1766, Pontiac agreed to a peace treaty that didn't settle anything: The Indians still refused to accept British rule, and the British were unable to completely subdue the Indians. The confederacy, however, had shown the British the power of tribes when united.

Tecumseh was well aware of Pontiac's uprising and appreciated its significance. He also was aware of the efforts of the Mohawk leader Thayendanegea, or Joseph Brant, leader of a pan-Indianism movement when Tecumseh was growing up. Brant wanted his confederacy to be strong enough to fight the white invasion of Indian lands and stop land grabs. In the end he failed to establish a powerful, lasting confederacy because of the difficulties of uniting independent Indian nations with distinct customs and ideas. Brant and Pontiac's ideas excited Tecumseh, encouraging him to build his own confederacy.

The centre of a growing pan-Indian movement was a place known as the Glaize, an old buffalo wallow at the junction of the Auglaize and Maumee rivers, about sixty miles southwest of present-day Toledo. French and English traders had built forts there that attracted Shawnee, Delaware, and Miami villages. The Glaize was home to two thousand people, mostly Indians, in 1792, the year that the Northwest's most powerful chiefs held a congress there to discuss how to resist American expansion.

There was much excitement about finally stopping the Americans. Following the congress, Shawnee chiefs travelled south to Alabama and Mississippi, asking other tribes to smoke a pipe of support for an alliance against the Americans. The

Indian confederacy movement was supported by the British in Canada, who supplied food and arms.

Tecumseh was not yet a powerful chief deeply involved in developing the confederacy. In fact, he spent much of his time hunting, which was his passion. He was known as the best of hunters and one who shared his catches without reservation. On one hunt he won a bet among Shawnee braves as to who could take the most deer in three days. None of the braves brought in more than ten each, but Tecumseh's count was about thirty.

Hunting was a dangerous occupation for the Northwest Indians of the 1790s. The territory was now travelled by American hunters, traders, and militias seeking Indian camps to destroy. Tecumseh's hunting in the spring of 1793 nearly ended in tragedy when the Shawnee were attacked by a band of Kentuckians.

Tecumseh was a light sleeper and on that night he slept beside the fire, while the others slept in tents or huts. The camp was approached by a group of Kentuckians led by Simon Kenton, the famous frontiersman and friend of Daniel Boone. The Kentuckians raised their flintlocks and poured musket balls into the sleeping quarters. Tecumseh jumped to his feet and grabbed his war club.

"Where are you, Big Fish?" he shouted to his blood brother Ruddell.

"Here I am," Ruddell replied from a tent.

"Then do your charge on that side and I will charge on this," yelled Tecumseh.

Tecumseh charged toward the Kentuckians, then presumably reloading their muskets. He clubbed one on the head and drove others back. Ruddell, meanwhile, jumped from the tent into the path of Simon Kenton himself. He fired at Kenton but his powder was wet and the shot fizzled while Kenton ran off.

After the fight, Tecumseh went looking for scattered horses and came across a straggling Kentuckian, who raised his gun to shoot him. Tecumseh charged him, overpowered him, and took him back to camp as a prisoner. Tecumseh and Ruddell then left again to round up more missing horses. They returned to find the prisoner murdered by the warriors who had remained in the camp. Tecumseh was very angry, Ruddell wrote later, and told the warriors it was cowardly to kill a man who was tied.

The Glaize, as an economic and diplomatic centre for what remained of the Ohio Country Indians, was not to be ignored by the Americans. President Washington, wanting to avoid more slaughters of his forces, established the Legion of the United States, a new military force commanded by General "Mad Anthony" Wayne. Wayne established a facility that provided the United States Army's first basic training program. Washington dispatched Wayne and his army to the Ohio frontier late in 1793, with orders to build Fort Recovery on the exact spot where St. Clair's army had been crushed. The idea was to demonstrate that the U.S. could recover from the humiliation and teach the Indians a lesson.

Wayne, in command of forty-six hundred troops, marched out of Fort Washington (Cincinnati) in the latter part of 1793, led by Chickasaw and Choctaw scouts. He planned to build forts and fight any Indians he could find along the way. The Indians had no intention of waiting for him to outnumber them. They attacked a supply group, killing twenty-soldiers but suffering heavy losses themselves. The attack resumed the next morning but the Indians were driven off.

Wayne almost didn't make it to Fort Recovery. On August 3, 1794, a tree fell on his tent and knocked him out cold. Unfortunately for the Indians, he quickly recovered and set plans for the rest of his campaign. A couple of weeks later he was beyond Fort Recovery and ready for a major battle at the Glaize.

As Wayne's army approached, the Indians set up a defensive position. They picked a spot on the Maumee River where a wind storm had knocked down large trees (possibly the same storm that put the tree down on Wayne's tent a couple of weeks earlier). The Indians figured that the fallen timber would slow the Long Knives' advance.

The Indians held a battle council on the eve of what was to be the Battle of Fallen Timbers. Tecumseh was there as a warrior, but the two main generals were the leaders of the victory over St. Clair — Blue Jacket and Little Turtle. There was argument over whether a battle should be fought the next day. Little Turtle was opposed, but he was overruled by the stronger influence of Blue Jacket, who was famous on the frontier as a warrior with many battles going back to Point Pleasant, twenty years earlier. The Indians had fifteen hundred warriors that included Ojibwe, Wyandots, Mingos, Potawatomis, and some Canadian militia. Wayne had them outnumbered.

Tecumseh commanded a party of Shawnee that included his brothers Lalawéthika and Sauawaseekau, and Stephen Ruddell. They were part of an advance guard when the fighting started. They rose out of the grass and knocked down six Americans, forcing the enemy backward. The new American army was trained, however, and they counterattacked. Tecumseh's gun jammed. He urged everyone to stand and fight, shouting for someone to lend him a gun and he would show them how. He was given a fowling piece, but soon an American counterattack was upon them with a flanking cavalry flashing long sabres.

The battle was lost but Tecumseh and his men fought with typical Shawnee tenacity. The Indians could not hold against the Americans. Some of their fighters were delayed returning from getting supplies at Fort Miami, the British post four miles away. Tecumseh ordered some followers to take a stand in a thicket. They fired into the advancing soldiers, but were soon forced to join a general retreat down the Maumee River. Sauawaseekau was left dead in their wake.

The retreating Indians reached the safety of Fort Miami, only to find the gates closed. They clamoured to get inside for protection against the pursuing Americans. Peering over the stockade wall was Major William Campbell, the British officer commanding the small garrison. He had a huge dilemma: if he let his Indian friends in, he risked touching off a new war between Britain and the United States. He pondered whether it was worth starting a war to protect his Indian allies. He looked down at warriors gathered outside the gates and shouted, "I cannot let you in! You are much too painted my children" — a reference to face and body paint worn for battle.

The warriors had no choice but to keep retreating downriver to Swan Creek, where the women and children had been sent for protection. Wayne's army did not pursue them but it destroyed the villages and crops at the Glaize. Once again the tribes were homeless and without food. As winter approached they were forced to turn to British charity to keep fed and warm.

Major Campbell's refusal to let the warriors into the fort was not the first time the British had turned their backs on their Indian allies. And it wouldn't be the last, as Tecumseh would discover in years to come. The incident sickened him. He had little respect for the British, but felt that they needed each other against the Americans.

On the battlefield that day was someone whom Tecumseh would learn to respect, and who would one day benefit from the wishy-washy British support of its Indian friends. Tecumseh did not see him in the battle, but he was there, and he would be there at other major battles. He was a twenty-one-year-old American lieutenant named William Henry Harrison, son of a prominent Virginia political family. His father Benjamin's signature is on the Declaration of Independence, and he himself was destined for great things. Harrison had studied as a doctor, but had left the Virginia plantation society in 1791, to join the army and head into the Ohio Territory. He became Wayne's aide-de-camp and would rise to become the man who decided Tecumseh's future.

The defeat of the Indians at Fallen Timbers was not devastating to their numbers. They lost thirty to forty warriors against forty-four for the Americans. However, their spirit was badly wrecked. The closed gates of Fort Miami told them they were fighting alone.

Blue Jacket spoke of the locked gates years later: "It was then that we saw the British dealt treacherously with us."

Broken spirits eroded the confederacy that was critical in stopping the Americans. The Shawnee gathered at Swan Creek and survived on British rations. Before the end of the year, some tribes sent peace messengers to the U.S. military headquarters at Greenville, south of Fort Recovery. In January 1795, the great Blue Jacket headed a peace party to General Wayne, bringing some other confederacy leaders with him.

Large numbers of Indians gathered for treaty talks with Wayne in the summer of 1795. The Treaty of Greenville was signed August 3. One of the signers was Lieutenant William Henry Harrison. Absent were Tecumseh and many other Shawnee. He was doing what he often did in times of Indian setbacks — hunting and reflecting.

The treaty saw the tribes cede much of the Northwest to the Americans, legally opening the land to settlers. In return they received some treaty goods and annuities. For this, hundreds of Shawnee and others, including Tecumseh's father and two brothers, had fought and died.

Blue Jacket visited Tecumseh to explain the treaty and gain his support, but the young chief refused to visit Greenville as a sign of his approval.

5

Descent into Sickness

As hard as he tried, Tecumseh could not escape the new American world. It descended on the Northwest Territory like the first winter snowfall, threatening to obliterate all traces of his former life. Fallen Timbers displaced his people. Their villages at the Glaize were destroyed, and the Shawnee split up once again, wandering in search of a territory on which to set their bark huts and plant their corn. Tecumseh took his followers to Deer Creek, just north of Dayton, in the spring following their defeat. Next spring, they moved to the Great Miami River, a bit farther west. The spring after that, they went to live among the Delawares at the headwaters of the White River, in what is now eastern Indiana.

As the new century approached, Tecumseh had spent almost five years trying to live a traditional life, away from white encroachment. There was relative peace, which allowed his people to hunt and plant crops. They were away from other Shawnee who had chosen to live among the settlers. Peace appeared about to be shattered, however, in the summer of 1799, and it prompted Tecumseh to emerge from his self-imposed obscurity.

Oddly, his emergence was as a diplomat, not as a warrior. Even odder, one man involved in Tecumseh's emergence was his old enemy, backwoodsman Simon Kenton. It started with gossip about Chickasaws from the south coming to take revenge on the Shawnee for something that had happened in the past. The Shawnee took the rumour seriously and mobilized, which panicked white settlers. The situation was serious enough that Kenton, who had moved to Ohio from Kentucky, and another settler wrote a letter to Shawnee chiefs through a French-Canadian who spoke the Indian language. The result was a meeting at which Tecumseh appeared as the principal speaker for the chiefs.

Tecumseh's speech was long, forceful, and eloquent, said people who witnessed it, but there was no explanation of why the chiefs chose him to speak. He lived independent of the Shawnee "establishment," had avoided signing any treaties, and did not particularly like the American intruders. He was known as a dynamic personality and strong orator, and those two reasons are likely why he was asked to speak.

Stephen Ruddell described Tecumseh, the orator:

> He was naturally eloquent, very fluent, graceful in his gestures, but not in the habit of using many words. There was neither vehemence nor violence in his style of delivery, but his eloquence always made a strong impression on his hearers.

Public speaking skill was highly valued in Indian communities. It came naturally because native North Americans had no written language. Every bit of communication, from recording their history to making plans for the future, was oral, and had to be clearly put and repeated many times to ensure that it was understood. Indian life was all about achieving consensus among the group, and talking things through was the best route to consensus. If you were a villager who felt passionately about a plan, concern, or cause, you had to be able to win people to your view with powerful word images.

Tecumseh was a master orator and the meeting was a success. War alarms were calmed and everyone went back to what they were doing. Tecumseh disappeared again into a traditional life of hunting and gathering. No written accounts of him appeared again until 1803, when another war alarm was raised.

In April of that year, a settler named Thomas Herrod was killed and scalped near his house, not far from Chillicothe on the Scioto River, the region where Tecumseh was born. Settlers were alarmed and some citizens of Chillicothe travelled west into Indian territory to find out who was responsible for the atrocity and perhaps prevent more hostilities. They came across a band of Indians that included Tecumseh, who told them his people were not involved in the killing and were keeping the peace. He agreed to travel to Chillicothe to speak to a gathering of settlers in hopes of allaying their fear.

Ohio had just become a state and its first governor, Edward Tiffin, attended the meeting. An eyewitness described Tecumseh's address:

> When Tecumseh rose to speak as he cast his gaze
> over the vast multitude, which the interesting

occasion had drawn together, he appeared one
of the most dignified men I ever beheld. While
this orator of nature was speaking, the vast
crowd preserved the most profound silence ...
he dispelled, as if by magic, the apprehensions
of the whites.

The eyewitness said that after meeting "the settlers returned
to their deserted farms, and business generally was resumed
throughout that region."

This meeting, and the earlier one arranged by Kenton, built
a new image of Tecumseh, the frightening warrior. He was
seen as an intelligent man of compassion and peace; someone
with the bearing and speaking talent to make others listen and
understand. He was commanding and persuasive.

Tecumseh was in his prime — thirty-one when he spoke
at the Kenton meeting, thirty-five when he addressed the large
Chillicothe group. Most everyone who saw him had the same
description: about five feet, ten inches tall, muscular; someone
who commanded respect but had a friendly disposition.

United States Army colonel William Stanley Hatch met him
and took time to write down a description:

> The personal appearance of this remarkable
> man was uncommonly fine. His height was
> about five feet, nine inches, judging him by
> my own height when standing close to him
> and corroborated by the late Colonel John
> Johnston, for many years Indian agent at Piqua.
> His face oval rather than angular; his nose
> handsome and straight; his mouth beautifully

formed like Napoleon, as represented in his portraits; his eyes clear, transparent hazel, with a mild, pleasant expression when in repose, or in conversation; but when excited in his orations; or by the enthusiasm of conflict, or when in anger, they appeared like balls of fire; his teeth beautifully white … he always stood very erect, and walked with a brisk, elastic, vigorous step; invariably dressed in Indian tanned buckskin…. He was then in the prime of life, and presented in his appearance and noble bearing one of the finest looking men I have ever seen.

A man of such description is naturally attractive to women. Tecumseh was, but had little interest in them. His life was lived mainly among men. He never hunted with women present, and his home life with women was not always happy.

The Shawnee generally were polygamous in Tecumseh's time, with the men taking as many wives as they wished and keeping them as long as they pleased. Divorce was common, and easy. Wives were simply told to leave, often for insignificant reasons.

Marriage customs began to change in Tecumseh's time. It was increasingly common for couples to live together without being married. "Every couple nowadays connect themselves and separate as suits their convenience or inclination," his brother Lalawéthika once told someone.

Tecumseh married and had relationships, but believed in having just one wife at a time.

He lived with a Cherokee girl while among the Chickamauga. It is likely they had a daughter. His first actual

Artist unknown. Field Museum, Chicago.

This portrait was once thought to be Tecumseh, but it is more likely his son, Paukeesau.

marriage was believed to have been at age twenty-eight when he took Mamate as a wife. They had one child, a boy called Paukeesau, who was placed in the care of his aunt Tecumapease, possibly because Mamate died. Tecumseh is said to have showed little interest in him, although there does not appear to be any evidence of why.

During his quiet years on the White River he tried two other marriages, but they were not successful. In one case, he accused the wife of serving his guests a wild turkey that was not thoroughly plucked, so he bundled up her belongings and sent her away. In 1802, he married a woman named Wabelegunequa (White Wing) and they lived together for five years before parting in 1807.

Certainly Tecumseh was not easy to live with. He was demanding and had heavy, arched eyebrows that sometimes gave him a severe look. He dressed plainly, without excessive decoration, but was fussy about his clothing. A white captive living among the Shawnee described him as fastidious. However, among almost everyone, Tecumseh was known as generous and humane; a man of integrity. He treated the aging and infirm with kindness, mending their wigwams when winter approached and giving them skins, clothing, and game. "From the earliest period of his life," recalled Mr. Johnston, an Indian agent in Ohio, "Tecumseh was distinguished for virtue, for a strict adherence to truth, honor, and integrity. He was sober and abstemious, never indulging in the use of liquor nor eating to excess."

The statement that he did not drink was not quite true. Ruddell recalled:

> He never or rarely ever drank ardent spirits
> to excess. When inebriated he was widely

different from the other Indians — perfectly good humoured and free from those savage ideas which distinguished his companions; and always reproving them for their folly.

Generosity was another attribute highly prized among the Shawnee, and other Indian communities. Sharing was important in Indian life. The most respected leaders were those who spread their prosperity among the less fortunate members of the tribe. It was often said on the frontier that no single Indian starved; if one starved, the entire tribe starved.

John Heckewelder, the missionary, was one of the first to observe Indian generosity, writing:

> The Indians are not only just, they are also in many respects a generous people, and cannot see the aged and sick suffer for want of clothing. To such they will give a blanket, a shirt, a pair of leggings, mocksens [moccasins], etc.

Tecumseh was known among Indians and whites as a leader who ensured that all his people, including the elderly and sick, always had the shelter and food they needed.

Some historians try to paint Tecumseh as the perfect man. He was not. He was impulsive and exhibited a level of pride bordering on arrogance. Certainly he could be ruthless, battling with relish and killing enemies with little thought. His ability to maim and kill with an old-fashioned war club is legendary.

In the first years of the 1800s, however, his war club and other battle tools got little use. He was content living out beyond the edge of the new "American civilization." He guided his followers, hunted, and lived a more or less traditional Indian life, a life he saw being buried by the advance of settlement.

The American settlements and farms consumed large tracts of forest. Animal populations were depleted, not only by shrinking habitat, but by more hunting. There were no supermarkets on the frontier and the food of the people was what they could take from the forest, or what they could raise. Fewer animals for skins, food, and trade meant more reliance on white trade goods. More reliance on trade goods meant less independence, which meant more assimilation into a white world for which they were not prepared. White customs and cultures were incomprehensible, and often damaging. White germs such as smallpox, for which the Indians had no built-up immunities, were devastating.

Tecumseh watched the Indian people slip into poverty and despair. A balm for their problems was also provided by the whites: alcohol, for which they had little tolerance. Whiskey brought violence and idleness, which increased poverty and desperation. Poverty and desperation forced the Indians to cede more land in return for more treaty annuities, which they used to buy more goods and liquor. American land speculators and settlers wanted their leaders to get even more land from the Indians. The government believed the future way of the Indian was to abandon the hunter-warrior life and assimilate into white society.

One of the country's most active land snatchers was the man Tecumseh never met on the Fallen Timbers battlefield: William Henry Harrison. He was the new governor of the Indiana Territory. Between 1802 and 1805, Harrison helped conclude seven treaties in which the Indians gave up huge

This painting of William Henry Harrison was done shortly before he became governor of the Indian Territory, circa *1800. From* Tecumseh; A Life *by John Sugden (1998).*

chunks of what would become the states of Indiana, Wisconsin, Missouri, and Illinois.

The tribes became hungrier and sicker in a shrinking world. They were fearful and some believed their own conduct had caused the Waashaa Monetoo to punish them. They needed to understand what was happening to them, and needed something in which to believe. It came to them through a most unlikely individual: Tecumseh's useless, shifty, and often drunk younger brother — the surviving triplet called Lalawéthika.

6

Casting Out Witches

Lalawéthika was an oddball among Tecumseh's siblings, in appearance and in actions. He was lazy and apparently uninterested in developing the skills of a hunter and warrior, perhaps because he was chubby, awkward, and not physically strong. He was homely; his turned down mouth exaggerated by a small moustache. His right eye was shut, permanently disfigured when he clumsily poked himself with an arrow. He dressed garishly, with ear decorations, a nose ring, and a large gorget at his throat.

The name Lalawéthika means "Noisemaker," and it fit because he was a loud and boastful talker. He possessed few skills and little purpose in his tribe. He was a true misfit, who drank alcohol and talked a lot to compensate for his shortcomings. He even described himself as "a very wicked man." One credit he did possess was knowledge of native medicine. He knew herbs and barks and roots, and when to prescribe them. He could even treat serious injuries, such as musket ball wounds, and knew how to call on the spirits for help in healing. This was enough to allow him to eke out a living, and would later help him achieve a purpose in life: as a messiah for the Shawnee and other Indians who had lost their traditional ways and any hope of finding them.

His indolent life turned around quickly and dramatically when he was about thirty. The Shawnee tell the story of him smoking his pipe and falling into a trance. His family presumed him dead and prepared him for burial. He woke up and said he had been visited by Waashaa Monetoo, who told him to deliver a message to the people: give up all white customs and goods and return to the traditional life. If they did this, he would drive the white settlers from Indian lands.

The change in Lalawéthika was astounding. He gave up alcohol and changed his name to Tenskwatawa, which means the Open Door. The idea of the name was that if the people followed the message from the Waashaa Monetoo, they would have an open door. He also became known as the Prophet.

He was not the only Indian to undergo such a transformation. A few years earlier and not far away, in the New York State area, an Iroquois named Handsome Lake had fallen into an alcoholic coma and his relatives had prepared him for a funeral. He had awakened and talked of visions about how the Great Spirit wanted his people to live. However, his visions varied from those of the Prophet in that Handsome Lake said it was acceptable to live in American-style houses and send children to American schools. He preached Indian revivalism with some assimilation into white culture.

The Prophet's transformation occurred about 1805, and he quickly developed a following. A year earlier, people had found him too drunk and unreliable to be a respected and dependable medicine man, but many began to accept him and his message. Disease was ravaging Indian villages, including Tecumseh's, and the people raised the possibility of witchcraft as the cause of their problems. Linking witchcraft to times of crisis was common among Indians. They were superstitious people with a powerful belief in spirits. Lalawéthika's religious transformation also had occurred elsewhere.

Many Indians believed witches were capable of flying long distances and that they carried ancient poison in their medicine pouches. This poison then spread the nightmares of disorders among the tribes. The Prophet's fame spread across the frontier, and the Delawares on the White River, who were desperate because of territory loss, hunger, and disease, asked him to come and cast out the witches among them.

A group of suspected witches, mainly older people with ties to the white community and white religions, were placed in a circle. The Prophet studied them carefully and with great flourishes declared them guilty or innocent. One of the first condemned, an old woman, was tied to a pole and suspended over a large fire. Screaming as her flesh burned, she said she gave her medicine bundle to her grandson, who was brought before the assembly, where he told an incredible story.

Yes, his grandmother had given him the medicine bundle and it had great power. He had used it to fly like a bird over southern Ohio, into Kentucky, over to the Mississippi River, and back in a few hours. The power of her medicine bundle had frightened him, so he had returned it to his grandmother. The Prophet was so taken aback by the story that he ordered the young man released. Others were not so lucky. Confessions were extracted through torture and the guilty were tomahawked and burned, or just tied to a stake and burned alive.

The commotion of Indian revivalism, witch hunts, and burnings soon reached the governor of Indiana Territory at Vincennes, a former French trading post where Governor Harrison occupied a mansion. Harrison was disturbed by the reports and wrote a letter to be hand-delivered and read among the Delawares. He believed that the upheaval among the Indians was a clever plan by the Prophet and Tecumseh to reorganize the tribes and get them under their control. He told the Delawares early in 1806:

> The dark, crooked and thorny one which you are now pursuing will certainly lead to endless woe and misery. But who is this pretended prophet who dares to speak in the name of the Great Creator? Examine him. Is he more wise or virtuous than you are yourselves, that he should be selected to convey to you the orders of your God? Demand of him some proofs at least of his being the messenger of the Deity. If God has really employed him he has doubtless authorized him to perform some miracles, that he may be known and received as a prophet. If he is really a prophet, ask of him to cause the sun to stand still — the moon to alter its course — the rivers to cease to flow — or the dead to rise from their graves.

What Harrison did not know was that Tenskwatawa the Prophet knew that a special celestial event would occur that summer. Harrison wanted to see a miracle, so the Prophet would give him one. He told his followers to appear in his village on June 16, to watch him make the sun stand still.

About noon on June 16, 1806, Tenskwatawa emerged from his lodge into the twilight caused by a solar eclipse and said, "Did I not prophecy truly? Behold! Darkness has shrouded the sun!"

As the sun returned, the crowds were convinced that Tenskwatawa the Prophet was indeed a messenger from Waashaa Monetoo. Who else could have brought Mukutaaweethee Keesohtoa, the "Black Sun," which portends war? Word of the Prophet's power and religious movement spread throughout Indian country. Tribes who were losing hope for the present and the future began to believe that following the Prophet's messages was an answer to their problems.

Soon after the eclipse, the Prophet revealed that the Great Spirit had ordered him to establish a village back in western Ohio, near Greenville. Greenville was inside the Greenville Treaty Line, on American soil, but the Prophet said this was the place where he was to conduct his spiritual revival of all Indians. The move from Indiana to Greenville caused much discomfort among new settlers, who feared Indian uprisings.

At Greenville, the Prophet became a magnet for Indian pilgrims who wanted to visit him and hear his preaching. By 1807, his teachings were so popular that Indians from afar trekked to the Greenville area, passing other settlements en route. The movement of large numbers of Indians alarmed the white citizenry, and there were demands that the Prophet and his followers be removed from the area.

The American leaders were suspicious of the Prophet and his intentions for another reason. The British, with their Canadian colony just to the north, were into a dirty war against France's Napoleon. Fallout from British blockades of European ports was affecting neutral countries such as the United States. Tensions between Britain and the U.S., never much relaxed after the U.S. War of Independence, were increasingly felt along the Canada–U.S. frontier.

Americans believed that the British had created the Prophet phenomenon, or at least were encouraging it. Governor Harrison wrote to the Shawnee in Ohio, and called the Prophet a fool who spoke the words of the devil and British agents. He accused him of defiling Greenville, the sacred spot where peace was made in 1795. He told the Shawnee in a letter:

> My children, shut your ears, and mind him not, or he will lead you to ruin and misery.
>
> My children, I have heard bad news. The sacred spot where the great council fire was kindled, around which the Seventeen Fires and ten tribes of their children, smoked the pipe of peace that very spot where the Great Spirit saw his red and white children encircle themselves with the chain of friendship that place has been selected for dark and bloody councils. My children, this business must be stopped. You have called in a number of men from the most distant tribes … My children, your conduct has much alarmed the white settlers near you. They desire that you will send away those people, and if they wish to have the impostor with them, they can carry him. Let him go to the lakes; he can hear the British more distinctly.

Tecumseh and the Prophet saw such words as harassment and a threat of war, and decided to abandon Greenville. They would move west again, and establish a new town on Indian lands away from the Americans. It was not just the threats from the Americans that forced them to leave. So many Indian pilgrims visited Greenville that it was difficult to feed them. Settlement had diminished the hunting and it was not possible to continue supporting huge numbers of pilgrims.

Before he left, Tecumseh attempted one last initiative to convince the Americans that he wanted peace, and explained his views on Indian rights. A meeting was held in the fall of 1807, at Chillicothe, now the Ohio state capital. Leading chiefs such as Blue Jacket were there but Tecumseh, who was not viewed as a major Indian leader, dominated the talks. At one point he delivered a three-hour speech denouncing various treaties as fraudulent. He accepted that they could not be undone, but said the Indians would not surrender any more land without defending it. The Americans at the meeting, including the new Ohio governor Thomas Kirker, were impressed with Tecumseh's intelligence and convinced that he did not want war.

The meeting marked a change in Tecumseh and the Indian revivalism movement. Previously, the Indian view had been that land was provided to everyone by Waashaa Monetoo. No one owned it, so no one could sell it. There were no boundaries. Now Tecumseh compromised and spoke of Indian land and American land. He agreed to borders but made clear he would fight against any further encroachment. Also, his policy was that remaining Indian land belonged to all Indians, and no one group could sell it without approval of all.

To enforce his view, Tecumseh called for a stronger Indian confederacy that would defend the land and rights of all Indians. This was a tough sell, as was getting all Indians to agree on anything. Individual Indian tribes saw the world from their own narrow perspective. Tribal politics, varying customs, and historical differences needed to be pushed aside and replaced by one all-encompassing Indian perspective. It was an impossible task, but Tecumseh believed that one Indian nation was the only way to stop American expansion and to defend Indian rights.

Tecumseh's confederacy also needed to push aside older chiefs who had become complacent and lost their will to fight. These were the chiefs who had signed or accepted land treaties and now were referred to as government chiefs. They had become part of the American establishment.

The Shawnee at Greenville abandoned their bark wigwams in the spring of 1808, and Tecumseh, his brother, and their followers headed west, some on horseback, and some in newly-constructed canoes. They settled at a scenic spot along the Wabash River, three miles below where the Tippecanoe River joined it. Here the forests were still intact, and there was abundant wildlife and good fishing in the rivers. The Miami tribe had named the area Kethtippecanoogi, "place of the succor fish people," which had been anglicized to Tippecanoe.

A new village of two hundred bark houses appeared on a bank of the Wabash. A large council lodge was built, plus a medicine lodge and large building named House of the Stranger. It would accommodate pilgrims who came to meet and hear the Prophet. Fields cultivated for corn, pumpkin, and squash stretched out beyond the village. It was known to the whites as Prophetstown.

Tecumseh had had no formal role in his brother's religious revival, but now he intended to use its popularity to help build a new pan-Indian political-military alliance. With the move back to Indiana, he would travel more, promoting and recruiting for a renewed confederacy.

One of his first trips out of Prophetstown was back to Ohio, to speak to the Shawnee and others at Wapakoneta on the

Auglaize River. At the Wapakoneta council was his boyhood friend, Stephen Ruddell, who had become a Baptist missionary after being returned to his family. Because he was still fluent in Shawnee, Ruddell was asked to translate a letter to the chiefs from Governor Harrison of Indiana. Tecumseh stood up, walked over to Ruddell, ripped the letter from his hands, and threw it into the fire. He announced that if Harrison had been there, he would have thrown him into the fire.

There was no chance that Harrison could have been there because he was at Fort Wayne, in the northern Indiana Territory, busily working against the interest of the Indians. He was negotiating a treaty to take roughly three million acres of land, much of it along the Wabash, for less than two cents an acre. Harrison needed more Indian land to complete Indiana's march to statehood. In the spring of 1809, Indiana Territory had been divided to create Illinois Territory, from which the states of Wisconsin and Illinois would eventually be created. However, the splitting off had lessened the Indiana Territory and population was one of main criteria for statehood. More land, more settlers, then statehood.

The treaty negotiations had been approved by James Madison, the new U.S. president. But he had set conditions, the most important being that all Indians with claim or pretended claim to the land were present, and that the treaty did not excite any Indians or cause any undesirable effects. For some reason, Harrison felt he did not have to obey the president of the United States and entered into a shameful negotiation at Fort Wayne. He packed the meetings with half-starved Indians who needed more annuities, and excluded some Indians who had claim to the land.

The Treaty of Fort Wayne was signed September 30, 1809. It was so blatantly unjust that it upset Indians who had been friendly to the Americans. Even some Americans saw the treaty as unjust, and they feared it could push the Indians into the arms of the British if war broke out again. It enraged Tecumseh, but it was a complete vindication of his efforts to halt American expansion.

If Harrison could have known the effects of the treaty on Tecumseh, he might have reconsidered it. Tecumseh now knew there was no dealing with the Americans. Words would not stop them; only the musket ball and war club would.

During the religious revival, Tecumseh had stayed in the shadows, agreeing with some of his brother's views, not necessarily agreeing with others. It was the Prophet's movement. Now, having tasted the bitterness of the Fort Wayne Treaty, Tecumseh stepped from the shadows to the forefront and turned the revival into a political-military movement to stop the takeover of Indian lands. Tecumseh's plan was to have the Fort Wayne Treaty reversed, and to stop civil or village chiefs from signing more land treaties. The power of the Indian movement now rested with the war chiefs, and all Indians had to agree to any land treaties.

Prophetstown filled with visiting Indians in the spring of 1810. Potawatomis, Kickapoos, Sacs, Foxes, dissidents from Delawares and Miamis, and even Ottawas and Chippewas from farther north, came to the village to talk about Tecumseh's confederacy. Many were younger warriors who had lost faith in the old government chiefs.

Tecumseh did not want to begin hostilities until he had completed building the confederacy. The treaty at Fort Wayne and subsequent talk had heated the blood of young warriors and no one could control all their actions. As summer approached there were clashes between small groups of Indians and settlers. Governor Harrison wanted to cool the situation and sent a messenger to address the Prophet at Prophetstown.

The messenger, a Frenchman named Joseph Barron, was brought before the Prophet and an assembly of Indians from many different tribes. The Prophet immediately called him a spy and told him to look down at his feet to see his grave. Then, Tecumseh entered the scene and took charge, asking Barron what he wanted, and assuring him that he would not be harmed.

Barron delivered the message from Governor Harrison, who still thought the Prophet was in charge. The message accused the Prophet of being an enemy and warned of the dangers of starting a war, even with the support of the British:

> Our Blue Coats [regular army] are more numerous than you can count, and our hunting shirts [militia] are like the leaves of the forests or the grains of sand on the Wabash. Do not think that the Red Coats [British] can protect you. They are not able to protect themselves. They do not think of going to war with us. If they did, in a few moons you would see our flags wave on all the forts of Canada.

Harrison's message offered to discuss the Indians' view of the Fort Wayne Treaty at his headquarters in Vincennes. Or, they could go to Washington to discuss their complaints with the Great Father. The latter suggestion was an often-used American ploy: bring Indians to Washington and dazzle them with the city and meetings with the president.

Barron and Tecumseh talked privately and began a negotiation for Tecumseh to travel to Vincennes to meet Harrison. It promised to be a historic meeting between two titans fighting for control of a large chunk of the Midwest. Harrison later attached a condition to the meeting; Tecumseh was to bring only a small group to Vincennes. He was no fool, and knew the Indian trick of feigning friendship while planning ambush.

Harrison then saw that in dealing with the Prophet, he had been talking to the wrong man. Through informants and messengers he realized that the genuine power in the Indian movement was Tecumseh. The realization was sudden and alerted the governor that he was dealing with a clever and powerful adversary. He acknowledged this in a letter to the Secretary of War in Washington:

> This brother is really the efficient man — the
> Moses of the family ... He is described by all
> as a bold, active, sensible man, daring in the
> extreme, and capable of any undertaking.

Harrison was a hard, calculating, and intelligent man. Now he had added to his portfolio one of the most important principles of warfare: know and respect your enemy.

The meeting was set for August and on the twelfth, an impressive flotilla of eighty canoes stopped at Fort Knox, just three miles north of Vincennes. The fort commandant described the scene in a letter to his wife:

> They passed this garrison, which is three
> miles above Vincennes, on Sunday last, in
> eighty canoes; they were all painted in the
> most terrific manner: they were stopped at the
> garrison by me, for a short time: I examined
> their canoes and found them well prepared for
> war, in case of an attack. They were headed by

the brother of the Prophet, (Tecumseh) who, perhaps, is one of the finest looking men I ever saw. About six feet high, straight, with large, fine features, and altogether a daring, bold looking fellow. The governor's council with them will commence to-morrow morning. He has directed me to attend.

The next day produced an intellectual clash, the likes of which was seldom seen on the North American frontier. The two men representing the two cultures battling for control of the Northwest finally met each other, and both realized they had met their match.

Harrison had ordered his people to set up the meeting on the portico of his mansion. Seats were strategically arranged for the comfort of all. Army officers, judges, and some citizens were there to view the proceedings. Tecumseh's people had encamped in a nearby Indian village. He arrived at the governor's house with forty warriors. He approached the portico to within about fifty feet, and then suddenly stopped, like a deer sensing something is not quite right.

The governor sent out an interpreter to tell Tecumseh to come and take his seat on the portico. Tecumseh objected, saying the portico was not an appropriate place. He pointed to a grove of trees. The governor had no objection, but noted that there were no seats out there. Tecumseh said there should be no objection to reposing on the bosom of mother earth. Harrison yielded the point, but ordered benches and chairs brought out to the grove. The Indians sat on the grass.

Tecumseh wasted few words getting to the point: His confederacy would resist all cession of land not accepted by all

Indian tribes, who were now under one nation, and of which he was the leader. He admitted having threatened to kill all the chiefs who had signed at Fort Wayne, but that the power of the civil chiefs had been transferred to the war chiefs. In future, any chiefs proposing to sell land to the Americans would be punished:

> No tribe has the right to sell, even to each other, much less to strangers … Sell a country! Why not sell the air, the great sea, as well as the earth? Did not the Great Spirit make them all for the use of his children?

He accused the Americans of driving Indians from the east coast and now being intent on driving them even farther:

> You are continually driving the red people, when at last you drive them onto the Great Lake, where they can't either stand or walk.

Harrison's reply was not at all conciliatory. It was ridiculous to suggest that the Indians were one nation, he said. If the Great Spirit had intended them to be one nation, he would have taught them to speak in one tongue. The Miamis were the real owners of the Wabash lands ceded in the latest treaty, and the Shawnees had no right to interfere.

Tecumseh was enraged at what he heard, jumped to his feet, and began speaking hostile-sounding words. Most of the people there didn't speak Shawnee and become alarmed by Tecumseh's vehemence. A senior army officer told a lieutenant that there was going to be trouble and to bring up the guard. Tecumseh's warriors stood with tomahawks and clubs in their hands.

The council appeared about ready to end in bloodshed. Harrison jumped up and pulled out his sword. A minister in the crowd ran to Harrison's house and grabbed a gun with which to defend his family. Everyone was staring each other down when the guard arrived with raised weapons. Harrison ordered them not to fire and asked the interpreter to find out what was happening. What had happened was that Tecumseh, angered by Harrison's speech, had jumped up and denounced him as a liar. Harrison said Tecumseh was a bad man and ordered him and his Indians to leave the area immediately.

Some historians believe that Tecumseh planned the tense scene that day. He had hoped to intimidate the governor, but unexpectedly found Harrison ready to fight.

Tempers cooled and other, much calmer meetings were held over the next two days. They did not change the standoff between Tecumseh and Harrison, however. Tecumseh said he would resist the survey of the Fort Wayne Treaty lands and the accompanying settlement. If necessary, he would join the British against the Americans.

If there was to be war, said Harrison, the Indians should at least end the practice of cruelty against women, children, and prisoners. Tecumseh agreed.

Not long after the eighty canoes disappeared upstream on the Wabash River, Governor Harrison ordered the survey of the Fort Wayne Treaty land to proceed under the protection of soldiers. About the same time a great wampum belt calling for warriors to unite under Tecumseh's confederacy returned to Prophetstown. It was sent on to a British agent who delighted in seeing so many warriors planning to join a cause that would no doubt help the British.

Harrison had done what Tecumseh had predicted, and

some of the governor's own countrymen had feared — driven Tecumseh and his allies into the arms of the British in Canada.

Tecumseh had asked Harrison to place the Indians' case before the U.S. president. Harrison said he would, but that the president's views would be the same as his own. Tecumseh replied:

> I hope the Great Spirit will put sense enough into his head to induce him to give up this land: it is true, he is so far off he will not be injured by the war; he may sit still in his town and drink his wine, whilst you and I will have to fight it out.

Tecumseh's prophecy would come true three years later on a battlefield along the Thames River in Upper Canada.

7

Tippecanoe

War drums and bloodcurdling chants filled the night skies above the council fires at Prophetstown. There was great excitement about the inevitable war against the Long Knives. There was no possible compromise to settle the dispute between Tecumseh's Indian movement and the United States.

Tecumseh had put his case to Harrison passionately: American expansion, through illegal land treaties, had oppressed the Indian people by diminishing their hunting grounds and their culture. Harrison could not or would not understand that point. He had negotiated the land sales with the rightful owners of the land, and would fight to protect the new territory.

Harrison told the Indiana legislature in November of 1810:

> It is with regret that I have to inform you that the harmony and good understanding which

it is so much our interest to cultivate with our neighbors, the aborigines, have for some time past experienced considerable interruption, and that we have indeed been threatened with hostilities ...

The young warriors were anxious for battle now, but Tecumseh would not rush to war. He was a thoughtful general. His best chance of pushing the Americans back across their expanding treaty lines was a strong confederacy. Warriors from afar rode into Prophetstown, but the confederacy was not yet complete. Tecumseh had to visit others to recruit support until he was satisfied he had the strength to soundly defeat the Americans. His efforts so far had only been modestly successful; many tribes preferring the white man's treaty annuities over the horrors of the battlefield.

When the snow left in the spring of 1811, Tecumseh was on the move again, visiting tribes, often in secrecy because he did not want the Americans to know his successes or failures. During his absence, small parties of Indians brought terror to the Americans by stealing livestock and murdering a few settlers here and there. Followers of the Prophet stole a boatload of salt that Harrison had sent north as part of the annuity to Indians who had signed treaties.

Harrison now feared that Tecumseh planned to attack Vincennes, with up to one thousand warriors. He even calculated how long it would take the Indians to travel on horseback and by canoe from Prophetstown to Vincennes, where he did not have the forces necessary to hold off an attack of that size. He asked the War Department for reinforcements and for permission to attack the Indians if he felt it necessary.

Harrison was a cunning man who saw Tecumseh as a major impediment to creating great civilized states in the northwest. The American government preferred to simply assimilate Indians without further bloodshed, but Harrison now had the arms, soldiers, and commitment to do what he wanted: to eliminate the Indian problem, period.

He wrote to Prophetstown:

> Brothers, this is the third year that all the white people in this country have been alarmed at your proceedings; you threaten us with war, you invite all the tribes to the north and west of you to join against us.
>
> Brothers, your warriors who have lately been here, deny this; but I have received the information from every direction; the tribes on the Mississippi have sent me word that you intended to murder me, and then to commence a war upon our people. I have also received the speech you sent to the Potawatamies and others, to join you for that purpose; but if I had no other evidence of your hostility to us, your seizing the salt I lately sent up the Wabash, is sufficient.

Tecumseh had no faith in more talks, but decided to visit Vincennes again. It would be easy enough to stop there on his way south to recruit Creeks, Choctaws, Chickasaws, and others. Talking with Harrison would buy more time for building the confederacy.

Harrison agreed to the visit but told Tecumseh emphatically not to arrive with a large group of warriors:

> Brothers, you talk of coming to see me,
> attended by all your young men; this, however,
> must not be so; if your intentions are good, you
> have no need to bring but a few of your young
> men with you. I must be plain with you; I will
> not suffer you to come into our settlements
> with such a force.

Tecumseh did not care what Harrison would or would not suffer. He arrived at Vincennes in late July 1811, with a party of three hundred (mostly painted) warriors. The place was an armed camp, with much evidence of soldiers with muskets and bayonets, and eight hundred militiamen dressed in buckskin shirts.

The talks went nowhere. Harrison was adamant; no renegotiation of the treaties. Tecumseh said he was going south and would not be back before the next spring. He hoped no settlers would move into the treaty lands before he returned. Many Indians were gathering at Prophetstown and would need those hunting grounds to feed themselves.

If anything, the meetings had shown Harrison that Tecumseh was an opponent to be respected, feared, and, if possible, avoided. The day after Tecumseh left, Harrison wrote the War Department. His note was remarkable in two ways: it was a stunning tribute to Tecumseh and it hinted at Harrison's intent to take advantage of Tecumseh's absence to destroy Prophetstown:

> The implicit obedience and respect which
> the followers of Tecumseh pay to him,
> is really astonishing, and more than any
> other circumstance bespeaks him one of
> those uncommon geniuses which spring up

occasionally to produce revolutions, and overturn the established order of things. If it were not for the vicinity of the United States, he would, perhaps, be the founder of an empire that would rival in glory Mexico or Peru. No difficulties deter him. For four years he has been in constant motion. You see him today on the Wabash, and in a short time hear of him on the shores of Lake Erie or Michigan, or on the banks of the Mississippi; and wherever he goes he makes an impression favorable to his purposes.

He added:

He is now upon the last round to put a finishing stroke to his work. I hope, however, before his return that that part of the fabric which he considered complete will be demolished, and even its foundations rooted up.

Harrison's plan to attack Prophetstown in Tecumseh's absence could not be concealed. There was talk and preparations at Vincennes. Word reached the Prophet and he was deeply concerned. Tecumseh had worked hard to restrain young hot heads from touching off a conflict at the wrong time. Before leaving, he warned Tenskwatawa to avoid trouble until his return.

The Prophet turned to his gift of the gab for help. He wrote Harrison, assuring him of his peaceful intentions, and that he would try to comply with Harrison's demands to return livestock stolen in raids and deliver Indians who had murdered some whites that summer. He knew he was unable to do that. The raids had been conducted by warriors acting independently, and while he was trying to soothe the governor, more horses were stolen and shots fired at whites.

Harrison was not to be smooth talked. He began marching troops north out of Vincennes in early October. En route, Indians fired at one of the army's sentinels, seriously wounding him. Word reached Harrison that the Prophet had announced that he had taken up the tomahawk.

To Harrison's credit, he made another effort at diplomacy, sending twenty-four Miami chiefs to talk to the Prophet. They were to tell him to return stolen horses and deliver killers of whites, or at least provide proof that the killers were not under his control. The chiefs did not return and Harrison believed they had joined the Prophet as followers.

When the army neared Prophetstown, riders sent by Tenskwatawa appeared and asked for an armistice until the following day when talks could be arranged. It was a typical Tenskwatawa trick but the army made camp for the night, although Harrison ordered everyone to sleep in their clothes and with their muskets at their sides.

At about four a.m., Harrison was pulling his boots on and talking to officers in his tent. An orderly stood ready to sound reveille to awake the troops. Suddenly, a shot exploded in the darkness. A soldier had spotted an Indian creeping upon the camp and had shot him. The shot was followed by a chilling war cry and the Indians attacked the camp from all sides.

The Prophet's attack plan, agreed upon at a council the night before, was to creep into the camp and kill Harrison. If an alert sounded, the warriors would watch for Harrison to mount his light grey horse, and then kill him. As the first shots rang out, Harrison ran from his tent and mounted the first horse he saw. His chief aide, Colonel Abraham Owen, rushed to a light-coloured horse. Warriors were waiting near the horse believed to be Harrison's and killed the colonel on the spot.

The amount of gunfire was severe. It started from one area then came from all sides of the camp. The American army regulars were green and untested by battle, and it appeared the Indians would deal them a blow similar to what they had given St. Clair some years before.

The alert sentry who shot the creeping warrior wrecked the Shawnee battle plan. Their assaults were fierce but localized and not fully coordinated. Most of the fighting was in the dark, with the Americans simply trying to stop the Indians from breaking through the defensive lines.

The Prophet was not part of the battle, and watched it from a small hill nearby, where he performed some mystic rite and sang war songs. The night before, he had told his warriors not to fear the American musket balls because Waashaa Monetoo would have them fall spent at their feet. Also, that the Great Spirit would ensure that the warriors would see as if it was daylight, while the Long Knives would struggle in thick darkness. Partway through the battle, messengers climbed the hill to tell the Prophet that his warriors were falling. He told them to fight on. Waashaa Monetoo would soon look after them, he said, and then resumed a louder and wilder version of his war chant.

When daylight returned Harrison counterattacked and began pushing the Indians back. It became apparent that the Prophet's magic was not working. The Indians began to lose faith and fall back. When the turmoil was over, Harrison had 188 dead and wounded, the Indians perhaps 120. Harrison's forces had roughly one thousand troops, regulars, and militia, while the Indian force had been estimated at perhaps four hundred.

The victory was considered Harrison's but he had lost 20 percent of his fighters, was 155 miles from home, and had little food. He was open to another attack. The plan had been to destroy Prophetstown, but Harrison decided that he must head home.

Late the following day, cavalry was sent to scout Prophetstown. Surprisingly, they found it abandoned except for one injured and elderly Indian woman. The Indians had gone for two reasons: they realized the American force was much larger and stronger than the Prophet had said, and they were short of ammunition. The soldiers collected foodstuffs and supplies they might use, then burnt the town. In terms of warfare, the Indians had nothing to be ashamed of. They fought with religious fervor, and with more ammunition and practical leadership they might have devastated Harrison's army.

Blame for the outcome fell on the Prophet. His followers held him responsible for their comrades who fell in the battle.

"You are a liar," one of the survivors yelled at him after the battle. "You told us that the white people were dead or crazy, when they were all in their senses and fought like the devil."

Tenskwatawa said Waashaa Monetoo had refused his prayers because his wife was menstruating and had contaminated his ceremony and incantations. Some followers bound him with cords and threatened to kill him. He was spared when they reconsidered that he was a holy man and killing might bring more disaster upon them.

The Prophet's magic was gone. His cunning and quicksilver tongue could not restore his powerful influence on the people. He had been impetuous and lacked good judgment. Without his brother's sound counsel he had crashed the Indian movement. His people dispersed, some settling nineteen miles away. They now faced a winter without their granaries or cooking kettles, and with little ammunition to hunt game.

Tecumseh heard nothing of the Prophetstown disaster during his amazing southern tour. His journey covered roughly three thousand miles into territories that later become ten states. As always, the success of his mission depended on whom he visited. Some tribes simply accepted the status quo and had no fire left for fight. Others considered Tecumseh's speeches carefully, while many others were unsure what was right. But Tecumseh was certain that his constant hammering at the need to build an anti-American expansion movement would forge his confederacy dream.

As usual, Indian superstitions played a role in the recruitment campaign. Early in 1811, a gigantic comet brightened the skies over parts of Europe. By summer it glowed on the edge of the North American night skies. In October, while Tecumseh visited the Creeks, it was bright enough to create a glow over the forests at night. Tecumseh pointed to it as an omen boding ill for his enemies.

The comet appeared over Creek country as Tecumseh arrived, and faded when he departed. The Creeks considered this, and the name Tecumseh, which to them meant Shooting Star. There was only one conclusion: this was indeed a powerful man blessed by the spirits.

When Tecumseh left the south to return home, there was another important sign. December 16, 1811, the New Madrid earthquakes shook Arkansas and Missouri. They were so strong that they rang steeple bells in Charleston, South Carolina. Stories developed that Tecumseh, before leaving the southern tribes, had said that he would stamp his feet or clap his hands and make the earth shake.

The earth did shake when he approached the Wabash-Tippecanoe region, and learned of the Prophetstown disaster. His rage at his brother and Harrison increased when he learned that the Long Knives dug up Indian graves, leaving bodies scattered on the ground to rot — an insane act of revenge. When he met Tenskwatawa, he scolded him severely and bitterly. The brother's explanation of what went wrong, which no doubt included the story of his wife's menstruation, enraged Tecumseh. He grabbed Tenskwatawa's hair, shook him viciously, and threatened to kill him.

It was a grim winter for Tecumseh and his people, who resettled Prophetstown. It was made grimmer when Tecumseh messaged Harrison saying he wanted to talk with the president in Washington. Harrison wrote back his approval, but said Tecumseh was to go as an individual, not as a leader of a group. Going alone would have made Tecumseh look like a defeated man without followers, a man at the mercy of the United States. He had no intention of doing that and never communicated again with Harrison.

Early in March, the peace of the frontier was disturbed once again by Indian raids. Several families were murdered on the Wabash and Ohio rivers. In May, twelve tribes held a grand council along the Mississiniway, a branch of the Wabash. The council professed peace and condemned the raids on the settlers. Tecumseh spoke to the council several times, saying he never advised anyone to attack the settlers, and that his views were misrepresented by the whites and Indians who sold land that did not belong to them.

Having brothers from other tribes speak against him added to the hurt and fury Tecumseh was suffering because of Harrison's attack on Prophetstown. He saw only one choice: he would travel

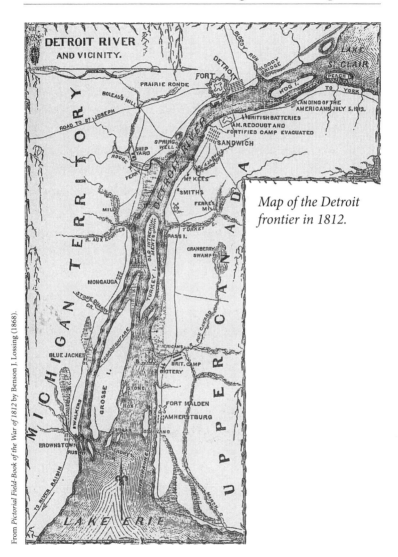

Map of the Detroit frontier in 1812.

From *Pictorial Field-Book of the War of 1812* by Benson J. Lossing (1868).

north to Canada and fulfill his prediction that Harrison's actions would drive him into the arms of the British.

His confederacy boasted thirty-five hundred northern warriors willing to fight. The time had come for all out war with the land grabbers of the United States. He rode north with a small party to consult with the British at Amherstburg, across the Detroit River in Upper Canada. He was confident that he now had the resources and the plan to drive the Americans from Indian country. What he didn't know as he rode was that Waashaa Monetoo was really smiling upon him then.

In June 1812, as Tecumseh headed for Canada, the United States declared war on Britain and its Canadian colony. Now Tecumseh would have his confederacy, plus British allies, in the war to recover his homelands.

8

War Comes to Canada

War dancing was already underway at Amherstburg when Tecumseh arrived. Campfire light flickered across warrior faces and bodies, painted in ferocious colours ranging from black and vermilion to blue and white. They were stripped to breechcloths and moccasins, and many had their heads shaved into Mohawk hair strips that bristled like porcupine quills.

News of war had reached the British settlement on the east bank of the Detroit River. Tecumseh had planned a few more finishing touches to his confederacy before waging his own war against the Long Knives. Now his war was part of the war to defend Canada against an inevitable U.S. invasion.

War tensions had been growing for years, and Tecumseh's and other Indian uprisings had been part of the reason. The Americans were fed up with having their expansion west blocked by Indians, encouraged and supplied by British Canada.

Also, the U.S. was angered by free trade restrictions placed by Britain in its war against Napoleon, and the British stopping of U.S. merchant ships to press into its naval services sailors whom it still considered British citizens.

War hawks in the U.S. believed it would be a short, easy war. All they had to do was invade Canada, capture the main forts, and the country was theirs; the problems with the British and the Indians would be ended. But it was not that simple and Tecumseh, now gathering Indian support around him in Amherstburg, would be one of the reasons why it wasn't.

Amherstburg was a village roughly twenty miles downriver from Detroit, the way the crow flies. When Tecumseh arrived at the end of June 1812, it was an important holding for the British, who gave up Detroit as part of the settlement of the American Revolutionary War. It sat where the river widened into Lake Erie, so it was a strategic port on the Great Lakes. The British had a military garrison called Fort Malden and a naval ship yard there, plus the headquarters for its important Indian department, whose job it was to cultivate allegiance of the Indians south of the Great Lakes. It was this department that had the Americans fuming at what they considered interference in U.S. internal affairs.

It was critically important for the British to hold the support of the Indians. This was a big job and much of the work fell to Tecumseh, who had to gather the Indians, hold them together, and then lead them into battle when the shooting began. Keeping the Indians unified was constant, frustrating work because the tribes had a history of switching allegiances depending on which side was winning. Tecumseh wanted no part of this back and forth, and made clear his position when he was invited to a council fire to discuss Indian neutrality at Brownstown, across the river from Amherstburg.

"No," he told the council. "I have taken sides with the King, my father, and I will suffer my bones to bleach upon this shore, before I will re-cross that stream to join in any council of neutrality."

Both the Americans and the Canadians were potential losers. The war was not supported throughout the fledging U.S. New Englanders had important trade ties with England and didn't want war to disrupt their business. In Upper Canada, many of the residents were immigrants from the U.S. who didn't want to fight their friends, neighbours, and family. Also, the U.S. population was much larger, much stronger, and had the war resources to overwhelm the Canadians.

Many Upper Canadians were so frightened that they talked of not resisting the invasion so that the Americans would treat them more favourably. The talk was so fearful that Isaac Brock, the British administrator of Upper Canada, suspended the legislature in York, now Toronto, and declared martial law, noting, "Most of the people have lost all confidence. I, however, speak loud and look big."

Amherstburg was the main Canadian defence on the Detroit River frontier, and it was not impressive. Fort Malden at the north end of the village was a bit dilapidated, but frenzied efforts were underway to reinforce the palisade, mount cannons, and deepen the ditch around it. The military consisted of roughly three hundred regular soldiers and perhaps six hundred militia, some of who were at Sandwich, the present-day Windsor, across from Fort Detroit.

The invasion came on July 12, 1812. The U.S. forces marched out of Fort Detroit and crossed the river by boat to Sandwich, where the residents fled or offered to help the Americans, led by Brigadier General William Hull, who was also the governor of

Michigan Territory. The Americans pitched camp on the farm of Jean Baptiste Baby, and General Hull took over the newly-built Baby mansion.

It was all as easy as everyone had expected, with Hull's army overrunning the country surrounding Sandwich. Even Tecumseh, in his heart of hearts, expected Amherstburg to be captured. Hull entered the country as a supposed hero, telling Canadians that he was liberating them from the oppressive British. He also proclaimed that they must abandon their Indian allies, a statement that said much about what was going on inside his head.

> No white man found fighting by the side
> of an Indian will be taken prisoner. Instant
> destruction will be his lot.

That statement revealed Hull's secret: He saw the Indians as savages and was terrified of them. It was a fear that would lead to his downfall.

The Americans began the march on Amherstburg, capturing the bridge at Rivière aux Canards (Canard River) just north of the village. A major battle was expected there the next day, and Tecumseh's Indians and volunteers sped to the scene. When they arrived, they were shocked to find the Americans were not there. Instead of pushing on to capture Amherstburg, the Americans had abandoned the bridge and were trekking back to Sandwich.

It was one of the more remarkable incidents of the war. General Hull was sixty years old and filled with doubts. Every opportunity appeared to him as a difficulty. He worried that there were more Canadian defenders than there really were. He worried about having his communication lines back to Ohio cut. He worried about the ferocity of Tecumseh's warriors. He was frozen by doubts and, instead of taking Amherstburg, he decided to wait for more Canadian militia to desert. His hesitation crippled the morale of his own troops, giving Tecumseh and the Canadians a desperately needed shot of hope.

When the American force turned back from the Canard River, it was harassed by Tecumseh's warriors in a series of small skirmishes. Hull was so fretful he talked of a plan to slip into Amherstburg to kidnap Tecumseh.

Tecumseh decided that if Hull wanted to worry about his Ohio supply-communications line, he'd give him good reason. In early August he crossed the Detroit River into Michigan, where the towns of Maguaga and Brownstown sat on the main road between Fort Detroit and Ohio. His plan was to block the path of a convoy of three hundred cattle and seventy pack horses carrying flour to feed Hull's troops.

Hull ordered one hundred and fifty troops south to River Raisin to meet the convoy and provide more protection. The Americans were fording Brownstown Creek when shots and war cries shattered the forest quiet. Tecumseh and twenty-five warriors sprang an ambush that scattered the panicking Americans. It was a humiliating defeat for the Long Knives. Outnumbered at least six to one, Tecumseh had driven off Hull's escort expedition, leaving eighteen dead, twelve wounded, and seventy missing.

The supply convoy remained stalled, so Hull sent out six hundred troops to push through Tecumseh's blockade. Tecumseh and the Redcoats, totalling two hundred men, sprang another ambush outside Maguaga. The firing was so intense that there was some confusion about who was who. The Redcoats fired at what turned out to be allied Indians creeping through the woods, and the Indians started shooting back. More confusion resulted in a misinterpreted bugle call that sent the Canadian forces into retreat. Tecumseh held firm in a cornfield, drawing much of the American fire, and was shot in the leg. Seeing his allies had left him, he ordered his warriors to fade into the forest.

The Americans had the confusion to thank for saving them. Still, they had eighteen dead and sixty-four wounded, compared with much lighter losses among the Indians and Redcoats. The fight drained some of their nerve. They feared another ambush and returned to Fort Detroit, leaving the supply train stranded.

The battles at Brownstown and Maguaga had important consequences. Tecumseh's ambushes had stopped two of Hull's mail runs and the captured letters were invaluable. One, from Hull to the War Department, revealed to Tecumseh Hull's fear of having his communications and supply line completely cut. In his mind, Hull saw himself surrounded. Indians were everywhere.

There was some basis for his fears. Two weeks earlier, he had received the news that the northern outpost at Fort Michilimackinac, 280 miles northwest of Detroit, had been taken by the British and Indians. Hull worried about being swarmed from the rear.

The supply convoy at River Raisin now had no hope of reaching Detroit until Tecumseh and his forces were cleared from the area. Hull, still occupying the Baby mansion in Sandwich, made the stunning decision to abandon his invasion of Canada. He started sending his troops back across the river to Fort Detroit, and made plans to clear the way for the supply convoy.

Tecumseh was back in Amherstburg tending his wound, and was no doubt pleased with his efforts. His diplomacy

Artist George Theodore Berthon.

Portrait of Major-General Sir Isaac Brock, Tecumseh's most effective British ally.

among the Indians in the Brownstown area had helped to gain the victories there, forcing Hull to stop the Canadian invasion. They had also helped to dispel the hopelessness apparent among the Canadians.

Amherstburg was safe for the moment and his fighters had gained a psychological edge. The Americans, on the other hand, were close to mutiny. Hull's own officers and troops now considered themselves commanded by "a frightened Old Lady." All that was needed to collapse Hull completely was for Tecumseh to be paired with a British officer who shared the Shawnee chief's vision and bias for boldness. That man, Isaac Brock, administrator of Upper Canada and head of its armed forces, just happened to be on his way to Amherstburg, and a date with history.

9

The Fall of Detroit

The room was lit by oil lamps, but the air was electric when Isaac Brock stepped forward to shake Tecumseh's hand. Here were two powerful men of action with the potential to change the course of the war. Brock was at least six feet, two inches tall, big-chested, and somewhat stout. His bearing radiated a boldness bordering on recklessness. He was a military man to the core, having enlisted as an ensign at fifteen, and serving in Europe with some of the world's best military leaders. His experience and talents qualified him for much more than a Canadian backwoods posting among frontiersmen and Indians.

Brock yearned for a more exciting assignment, telling his brother, in a letter the previous year:

> You who have passed all your days in the
> bustle of London, can scarcely conceive the

uninteresting and insipid life I am doomed to lead in this retirement.

"This retirement" had lasted ten years. He had shipped to Canada in 1802, with the 49th (Hertfordshire) Regiment of Foot, and spent the decade building up the colony's defences, and training militia for the long-anticipated war with the U.S. Ironically, a transfer to European duty, sought for so many years, had been granted, but he had turned it down because he felt committed to the defence of Canada.

Brock and Tecumseh were a stunning contrast in the same room: Brock, squeezed into his red military jacket trimmed with gold braid and buttons, exhibiting all the confidence and authority of a British Army major-general; Tecumseh, shorter and slimmer, in his buckskins, had a relaxed manner, but was no less prepossessed. Dissimilar in dress, culture, and backgrounds, the two were similar in their thoughts and actions. Each was a man's man and both preferred life among men; Brock was a confirmed bachelor, and Tecumseh spent little time with any woman.

The Meeting of Brock and Tecumseh. *Pen and ink drawing on paper, C.W. Jeffreys, circa 1921.*

Major John Glegg, an aide to Brock, later wrote about Tecumseh's appearance at the meeting:

> Tecumseh's appearance was very prepossessing: his figure light and finely proportioned; his age I imagined to be about five and thirty [actually he was forty-four]; in height five feet nine or ten inches; his complexion, light copper; countenance, oval, with bright hazel eyes beaming cheerfulness, energy and decision. Three small silver crowns, or coronets, were suspended from the lower cartilage of his aquiline nose; and a large silver medallion of George the Third ... was attached to a mixed coloured wampum string, and hung round his neck. His dress consisted of plain, neat uniform, tanned deerskin jacket, with long trousers of the same material, the seams of both being covered with neatly cut fringe; and he had on his feet leather moccasins, much ornamented with work made from the dyed quills of the porcupine.

Brock arrived at Amherstburg late the night of August 13, in response to Hull's invasion. His arrival was greeted by volleys of musket fire from Indians rejoicing in seeing reinforcements under the top Upper Canada general. Brock was not impressed by the loud welcome and told an aide to explain to everyone that munitions were short and powder should not be wasted. Half an hour later, the aide returned to Brock's quarters with Tecumseh, who heard the general's complaint about the celebratory firing and agreed that powder should not be wasted.

Brock told the chief he had fought the enemies of the king on the other side of the great salt water. He now desired "with my soldiers to take lessons from you and your warriors, that we may learn how to make war in these great forests."

Both men liked each other immediately. They were instinctive generals, aggressive battle planners; men who quickly received the respect of people they met. Legend has it that Tecumseh, excited that the British had sent a real man of action, turned, threw out his arm, and exclaimed, "Hooyeee. This is a man!"

Brock, no less impressed, later referred to Tecumseh as "the Wellington of the Indians," a reference to the famous Duke of Wellington who fought against France, and later defeated Napoleon at the Battle of Waterloo.

Brock had been cautioned by his boss, Sir George Prevost, governor of all Canada, to remain defensive and not risk battles with the Americans. There was sound reason for this: Canada had only 5,200 regular troops, 1,200 assigned to Brock. There were eleven thousand militia, but Brock estimated that only four thousand could be trusted to fight because he had witnessed mutinies and desertions among them.

Major-General Brock was a good soldier and followed orders; however, he was also one to follow his instincts. He judged that Hull was weak and afraid of the Indians. He felt that desperate times required desperate measures and decided on an aggressive offensive: he would attack Fort Detroit. Tecumseh and the Indians were rapturous. The next morning, Tecumseh told a council that finally the Great Father in Britain had awoken from his sleep and sent soldiers to drive back the Americans.

No time was wasted. On August 15, Brock, ever bold, sent General Hull an impudent message demanding that he surrender Fort Detroit. Hull, who only days before had occupied a strategic piece of Canadian soil, was startled. Having been so close to holding Amherstburg, he never expected to be pursued back to his home fort.

Brock's written demand for surrender was cleverly composed, and preyed on Hull's fear of the Indians:

> The force at my disposal authorizes me to require of you the immediate surrender of Fort Detroit. It is far from my inclination to join in a war of extermination; but you must be aware that the numerous body of Indians who have attached themselves to my troops, will be beyond my control the moment the contest commences. You will find me disposed to enter into such conditions as will satisfy the most scrupulous sense of honor. Lieut-Colonel McDonell and Major Glegg are fully authorized to conclude any arrangement that may lead to prevent the unnecessary effusion of blood.

The message struck at the centre of Hull's fear. Inside the fort were civilians, including his daughter and grandchildren. A short time earlier, Hull had wondered about a possible attack and in a moment of fear blurted out, "My God, what shall I do with all these women and children?!" However, he wrote back to Brock, bravely stating that he would fight and suffer the consequences.

Brock's officers, including Colonel Henry Procter, who would take over the western front from Brock later, were opposed to his attack on Detroit. Brock was not swayed, and after Hull's negative reply was received, British big guns at Sandwich started firing across the river at Detroit. The Americans returned fire with their twenty-four-pound cannons.

The assault on Detroit was set for the next morning. Brock pulled Tecumseh aside and asked him what kind of terrain he could expect around Detroit. Tecumseh pinned a roll of bark to the ground with four stones. He pulled out his scalping knife and etched a sketch of the countryside including hills, forests, rivers, swamps, and roads. Brock was mightily impressed.

At six o'clock the next morning the cannon fire resumed, and 330 Redcoats and four hundred Canadian militia in boats and canoes crossed the half-mile width of the Detroit River, landing unopposed. Anywhere from three to six hundred Indians under Tecumseh had crossed during the night, setting up in the woods at the Americans' flanks and rear.

The dawn attack was described by John Richardson of the Canadian militia:

> A soft August sun was just rising, as we gained the centre of the river, and the view, at the moment, was certainly very animated and exciting, for, amid the little squadron of boats and scows, conveying the troops and artillery, were mixed numerous canoes filled with Indian warriors, decorated in their half-nakedness for the occasion, and uttering yells of mingled defiance of their foes and encouragement of the soldiery. Above us again were to be seen and heard the flashes and thunder of the artillery from our batteries, which, as on the preceding day, was but feebly replied to by the enemy, while the gay flags of the *Queen Charlotte*

[British warship], drooping in the breezeless,
yet not oppressive air, and playing on the calm
surface of the river, seemed to give earnest of
success, and inspirited every bosom.

Richardson was a fifteen-year-old boy who lived with his
parents at Amherstburg. He had joined the militia as a gentleman
volunteer. He would fight in many battles before his capture at
the Battle of Thames in October 1813. He was imprisoned until
the war ended, and eventually became one of Canada's earliest
internationally known novelists. His war experiences provided
the grist for two of his best-known novels, *Wacousta* and *The
Canadian Brothers.*

Brock's strategy was to have the Americans come out from
the fort and engage in open battle. However, the Americans,
twenty-five hundred strong, remained barricaded inside. Brock
received the chilling news that a detachment of 350 Americans,
sent to find and escort the supply convoy that was still stranded
at River Raisin, was on its way back and very close by. Hull,
having received the demand for surrender the day before, had
quickly recalled the relief detachment to help defend against
Brock's attack.

The safest move for Brock was to return across the river.
Instead, he decided to attack before the River Raisin relief
column was upon them. He moved his command section
into a ravine about one mile from the fort and readied the
attack. Tecumseh surrounded the fort and took positions that
threatened the town. One version of the story is of Tecumseh
marching Indians back and forth to make Hull think there were
three to four thousand of them. There is no documented proof
that that's what happened, but later events confirm that Hull

feared the Indians were overrunning the outskirts of the town.

At ten o'clock that morning everything was ready for the attack to begin. Then, inexplicably, the Americans' cannons went silent and troops manning an advance battery outside the fort withdrew inside. A white flag appeared over the fort's wall. An American captain, who happened to be Hull's son, emerged carrying a white flag. The Americans had surrendered without a shot, except for the usual exchange of pre-battle long-range cannon fire.

One American officer told Hull, "Damnation! We can beat them on the plain. I did not come here to capiltulate. I came to fight!"

Brock and his troops were flabbergasted, but no more so than many of the American troops inside the fort. By noon, Brock and Tecumseh had marched into the fort to claim their prizes: Fort Detroit, the Michigan Territory, thirty-three cannons, a brig of war, a large amount of arms and powder, and 2,500 prisoners.

The capture of Detroit meant much more than goods and territory, however. It shattered the U.S. invasion plan, delaying another attack on Upper Canada's western front by at least a year. It also boosted the support of any Indians who were wavering over which side to join, and shook Upper Canadians from their defeatism. It was a huge blow to the United States. Some of the Americans inside the fort threw down their weapons in disgust, others broke into tears. Some were later released on parole, with promises to abstain from future fighting. Others were shipped to Montreal for future prisoner exchanges.

One prisoner, surgeon's mate James Reynolds, wrote in his journal:

> Who can express the feelings of a person who
> knows that Hull had men enough to have this
> place three times and gave up his post. Shame to
> him, shame to his country, shame to the world.

General Hull bore the full weight of the humiliation and anger that swept the American army and the public. He was released to return to Washington, where he was branded a coward and a traitor, and charged for court martial, which was held in Albany, New York, in January 1814.

A witness at the court martial painted a sad picture of a pitiful, old, and fearful man on the day that Brock and Tecumseh appeared at the Detroit gates:

> [T]he General selected the safest place in the fort
> for his seat, on an old tent on the ground and
> leaned against the ramparts between the guard
> house and the gate; his voice trembled when he
> spoke — he apparently unconsciously filled his
> mouth with tobacco, putting in quid after quid,
> more than he generally did; the spittle coloured
> with tobacco juice ran from his mouth on his
> neckcloth, beard, cravat and vest; he would rub
> the lower part of his face, which was apparently
> covered with spittle; he was repeatedly informed
> that the enemy were crossing the river, but he
> took no measures to oppose them, with which I
> am acquainted.

He was found guilty of cowardice, neglect of duty, and unofficer-like conduct, and sentenced to death by firing squad.

President James Madison, citing his honourable service in the Revolutionary War, commuted the sentence to a dishonourable discharge and having his name stricken from army records. To this day, he is the only American general ever sentenced to death by a court martial.

General Brock returned to York on August 27, where he was greeted as a hero. In barely three weeks he had suspended the legislature, travelled over three hundred miles to meet an invading enemy double his army's size, and had captured Detroit and a huge chunk of territory roughly the size of Upper Canada. All said, the capture of Fort Detroit was a critical element in Canada remaining a separate country from the United States.

Tecumseh's role was well-recognized by Brock. He wrote the British prime minister not long after the capture of Detroit:

> A more sagacious or more gallant warrior does
> not, I believe, exist. He was the admiration of
> every one who conversed with him.

There is a story that after the capture of Detroit, Brock took off his red sash and placed it around Tecumseh's body. Tecumseh gratefully accepted it, but was later seen without it. Brock, fearing he had done something wrong, had an interpreter ask about the sash. The explanation was that Tecumseh gave the honour to Chief Roundhead of the Wyandots, who he said was an older and more able warrior.

There also is a story that Brock, or some other British commander, commissioned Tecumseh as a brigadier general in the British Army. There is no evidence to support this, even though artists often paint Tecumseh dressed in a British uniform.

Tecumseh, in earlier days, was sometimes seen in white man's dress, such as a cloth hunting smock. But with the rise of his brother's religious movement he avoided white goods and was most often seen in the uniform in which he met Brock: fringed deerskin jacket and trousers.

Tecumseh was a diplomat who took care not to unnecessarily wound the feelings of any ally. He, however, had little interest in the future of Canada, or the British. He could care less about any white people, their titles and politics, or their geographical boundaries. The British would be satisfied with a draw in the war against the Americans. Tecumseh needed an all-out win. He was in the fight for one reason only: the restoration of his homelands in the Ohio Country.

Brock appeared to be one of the few who fully understood that. In his letter to the prime minister praising Tecumseh, he also wrote:

> They appear determined to continue the contest until they obtain the Ohio for a boundary. The United States government is accused, and I believe justly, of having corrupted a few dissolute characters whom they pretended to consider as chiefs, and with whom they contracted engagements and concluded treaties, which they have attempted to impose on the whole Indian race.

Brock's respect of and support for the Indians was powerful. Unfortunately, he did not live long enough to help Tecumseh realize his dream. As Brock turned his attention to another invasion at Niagara Falls, Tecumseh saw a storm cloud looming in the south. American troops and militia were being assembled to take revenge for the humiliation of Detroit, and to end the Indian uprising that just would not stop. Leading the storm was the new commander of the U.S. Northwest army, and the only American who seemed capable of any success against the Indians — Tecumseh's nemesis, William Henry Harrison.

10

Fort Meigs

In many ways the citizen militiamen, and even the new professional American soldiers, were no match for Tecumseh's warriors. U.S. soldiers in 1812 were professionally trained, more disciplined, and fought in cohesive units. Their numbers were usually greater than the Indians', and they certainly had better technology.

However, Tecumseh's fighters used their environment to great advantage. Their tracking skills gave them superior military intelligence. They did not require elaborate supply lines because they could live off the land. Their knowledge of the forests allowed them to use dash and dart fighting techniques, taking advantage of the close cover of windfalls, large trees, rocks, hills, and gullies. Their offence was deception and surprise, while their main defensive tactic was not to remain in a prolonged battle where every fallen warrior seriously weakened their smaller numbers. They fought spontaneously, making their own fighting decisions, free of rigid command and control.

The European style of battle was to line up rows of infantry in open spaces, then watch them be chopped down by musket volleys. European nations could afford that type of battle because manpower was unlimited. The small Indian populations could not, so they preferred close cover hit and run action, to which the Americans had to adapt. They learned the Indian fighting techniques well, but one-on-one, the Indian warrior was the superior fighter. One reason was that the American soldier was doing a job; the Indian fighter was doing what he was born to do.

What dissolved the Indian fighting advantage was the frontier fort. Forts, strategically placed and solidly built, were almost inpenetratable to Indian weapons: bow and arrow, war club, tomahawk, and the musket. They might try to pick off a few enemies through sharp shooting, setting the stockade on fire, or using ruse to gain entry. Without white army allies and their cannons and bombs, the Indians had little success against frontier forts.

As Tecumseh later noted at a war council in Amherstburg, "It is hard to fight people who fight like ground hogs."

Harrison's life work was now to completely squash the Indian problem while defeating the British. He had stepped aside after twelve years as governor of Indiana to become a commander in the war against Britain. One of his plans was to build a temporary fort near Lake Erie from which he could invade Canada. He picked the south side of the Maumee River, upstream from where it emptied into the southwest corner of Lake Erie, near present-day Toledo. He named it for Jonathan Meigs, governor of Ohio.

Fort Meigs was built during the winter of 1813, with the understanding that the British would view it as a major threat and attack it in spring. Its construction was supervised by one of the U.S. Army's best engineers. It was octagonal with eight block houses, picketed with timber and surrounded by ditches. It was built to house two thousand soldiers.

While Fort Meigs was being built, Tecumseh suffered through a winter of discontent. The leg wound he suffered outside Maguaga had not healed properly and he had lost the use of it for awhile. By Christmas it was recovering, but that good fortune was not enough to lift his sagging spirits. The summer of 1812 had not ended well for Tecumseh, in terms of the war. There had been important victories, but some incidents that left him with suspicions that the British alliance was not giving him the support that he expected.

The summer capture of Michilimackinac and Detroit buoyed the Indians, who then staged attacks throughout the Northwest. Fort Dearborn, near Chicago, was overrun, with most of the garrison being either killed or captured. Soon after, a huge body of Indians assembled near Fort Wayne and began ravaging settlements in that region. They tried to capture the fort but failed, so instead they surrounded it and called for the British and Tecumseh at Amherstburg to send reinforcements. General Henry Procter, Brock's successor when he left Amherstburg to command the Niagara front, agreed to reinforcements but sent them too late. The Indians at Fort

Wayne abandoned their siege when they learned that General Harrison was in the region with 2,200 men.

Procter had sent out Tecumseh and Redcoats led by Major Adam Muir, who arrived at the Maumee River only to hear that the Indians had abandoned the Fort Wayne attack. They had paused to consider what to do next when they learned that a large American force led by General James Winchester was coming in their direction and was only thirty-six hours away. Some problems, including hesitation and desertion of some of the Indians, led Muir to retreat downriver toward Lake Erie. Finally, he decided not to risk his artillery, loading it up and shipping it down the river and across the lake to Amherstburg.

The retreat without a fight disturbed Tecumseh. He had learned that many British officers, like Procter and Muir, and the Major Campbell who had locked the gates on him at Fort Miami, were not from the same mould as General Brock. Procter in particular did not have Brock's decisiveness or his rapport with the Indians. Tecumseh saw Muir's retreat as the result of the change of command, and it did not speak well for the future.

Worse still, Tecumseh received the painful news that General Brock had fallen at Niagara. The daring Brock personally led a charge to retake a critical gun position when the Americans streamed into Canada across the Niagara River. He was a prime target; on horseback with his cocked hat and red jacket with the bright gold epaulets. A marksman shot him in the wrist, but he pressed on until another bullet hit him in the breast. His dying words were reportedly, "Push on brave York volunteers." Today, the motto of Brock University in St. Catharines, Ontario, is "Surgite! Push on!"

Tecumseh would never meet another British officer to compare with Brock.

Brock's death and the nagging doubts about British commitment to fighting in tough situations left Tecumseh with much to ponder that winter of 1812–13. In the meantime, his brother the Prophet had gone off half-cocked again. In early September, the Prophet sent a war party from Prophetstown against Fort Harrison, near modern-day Terre Haute, Indiana. They tried to gain entry through a ruse, but the Americans didn't bite. They set fire to the stockade and laid down some musket fire on it, but the Americans held fast, put out the fires, and repulsed the attack.

The Prophet was discouraged by the attack, and the news that Harrison had soldiers sweeping the countryside and destroying Indian villages and crops. He hid his winter food supplies in the forests, but the American forces combing the countryside for Indian resistance found and destroyed them. The Shawnee now faced another hungry winter because of the Prophet's poor judgment.

Tecumseh certainly was not amused by all this as he completed his recovery. He continued to make plans for a spring offensive, and moved about from village to village to build support for the anticipated battles ahead.

While Tecumseh wintered, General Harrison was busily building Fort Meigs, and General Procter was at his desk in Amherstburg plotting a spring attack against him — it was important that he hit the new Fort Meigs early, before the Americans could stock it with reinforcements. During the night of January 19, 1813, Procter was awakened with the urgent news that part of Harrison's force had occupied Frenchtown, a village on the north bank of the River Raisin just thirty-one miles south of Detroit. Procter concluded that Harrison was planning to cross the ice from there to attack Amherstburg.

The Americans, including seven hundred Kentucky militiamen under General Winchester, had quickly overcome a weak British presence at Frenchtown, captured their stores, and established a base. Procter marched immediately on Frenchtown with six hundred Redcoats, six pieces of artillery, and seven hundred Indians led, in Tecumseh's absence, by Chief Roundhead. Procter caught the Americans totally unaware and unprepared on January 22. His artillery made short work of the battle and before long Americans were running for their lives through deep snow. Indians chased them down, splitting their heads with tomahawks and lifting their scalps. Winchester, still wearing a nightshirt, was captured and surrendered the rest of his troops.

Procter had dealt the Americans a vicious blow, but he decided to return quickly to Amherstburg in case the rest of Harrison's army was nearby. In the haste to return home, he left eighty sick and wounded Americans behind, waiting for sleds that would take them away the next day. The injured never made it to the sleds, however. After Procter left, fifty drunken Indians rampaged through Frenchtown, beating and tomahawking the sick and injured Americans, or burning them alive inside the buildings. Some bodies were tossed into the streets where they were torn apart by hogs.

Frenchtown was a massacre of huge proportions, the biggest battle ever fought on Michigan soil. Several hundred Kentuckians died, including nine militia officers, honoured by the Kentucky government by having counties named after them. Procter had departed before the massacre of the wounded, but he was the man in charge and was considered responsible for a savagery that would never be forgotten by the Kentuckians. Before long he would hear the cries of "Remember the Raisin" and feel the sting of the Kentuckians' revenge.

News of the Procter and Roundhead victory must have lightened Tecumseh's heart and raised his spirits for the spring campaign. However, for a warrior who always protected the sick and wounded of war, the news left a bitter taste.

Three months later, late in April 1813, Amherstburg again heard the pounding rhythms of war drums and was filled with painted Indians dancing their war preparations. Procter was ready to cross the lake and engage Harrison at Fort Meigs. Tecumseh, at the head of twelve hundred warriors, arrived April 28 at the mouth of the Maumee to join Procter, who arrived on lake boats with roughly one thousand Redcoats and Canadian militia. The British batteries opened fire on Meigs on May 1, while Tecumseh and his warriors surrounded the fort.

What no one outside the fort knew, however, was that Captain Eleazor Wood, the brilliant engineer who built Meigs, had thrown up a traverse the length of the inside of the fort. It was an earth mound twelve feet high and twenty-four feet wide. The American troops dug in on the back side of it, well protected from the British cannonballs and shrapnel. Captain Wood had even had tents erected along the front of the traverse, so that anyone peeking into the fort saw only canvas and not the new fortification.

The British hurled hundreds of red hot cannonballs and thousands of pieces of shrapnel at the fort for four days. Tecumseh's warriors climbed into trees and fired muskets into the fort. A few soldiers inside were killed, but the fort held firm. The Americans returned some fire but stayed hunkered in their traverse while Tecumseh fumed and began to bad mouth the British for their inability to knock down the fort.

Harrison knew that nine hundred Kentucky militiamen under General Green Clay were on the way to help him. They were floating down the Maumee River on barges and were a few miles away when they stopped because of darkness. Harrison sent a messenger telling them to come the rest of the way in the morning and to divide into two groups. One would hit and spike the British cannons, then retreat to the fort; the other should land upstream and attack the Indians surrounding the fort.

The first part of the plan worked well. The Kentuckians, led by Colonel William Dudley, captured and spiked the British cannons. The British were surprised, but the Kentuckians were so thrilled with their success that they did not fall back to the fort. They chased some warriors, who ran toward the British-Indian camp, where Tecumseh and the Redcoats were aroused by the gunfire. The exhilarated Kentuckians suddenly hit a wall of Tecumseh's forces, which pushed them back. Soon the Kentuckians were in full flight, many dropping under war clubs and musket balls, some throwing their weapons down and running for the river. Most did not make it. Dudley was one who didn't. The Indians tomahawked him, then scalped him and stripped skin from his body.

Only one-quarter of Dudley's eight hundred Kentucky militiamen scrambled across the river and into the safety of Fort Meigs. Two hundred twenty died under the weight of the warriors and roughly four hundred more were taken prisoner. Some of the prisoners met the same fate as their fallen comrades.

Tecumseh was surveying the field after the battle when he received word that a large group of Kentuckians had been taken to the remains of Fort Miami, an abandoned British post close by, and were being run through a gauntlet. He jumped on a horse and galloped to the old fort where he found scalped bodies littering the ground. Those who had survived the gauntlet were being slaughtered randomly.

There are several versions of what Tecumseh did upon his arrival. One has him jumping up on part of a wall, waving his tomahawk and daring anyone to touch one more prisoner. Another has him demanding of General Procter why he and his officers did not stop the slaughter.

"Your Indians cannot be commanded," Procter replied.

"Begone," Tecumseh shouted back. "You are unfit to command; go and put on your petticoats."

No one will ever know the exact words and actions of that scene, but enough witnesses were there to testify that Tecumseh did arrive, stopped the slaughter, and chastised Indians and British for cowardly conduct.

The savagery of the battle was described some years later by a British officer retelling his experiences in a London, England, magazine. He had visited the Indian encampment after the battle and had seen warriors rifling boxes and trunks taken from captured American boats. Warriors examined items of clothing, some trying on officers' uniform coats, others stumbling about in big, military boots, which were awkward on feet so accustomed to moccasins:

> But mingled with these, and in various directions, were to be seen the scalps of the slain drying in the sun, stained on the fleshy side with vermilion dyes, and dangling in the air, as they hung suspended from the poles to which they were attached, together with hoops of various sizes, on which were stretched portions of the human skin, taken from various parts of the human body, principally the hand and foot, and still covered with the nails of those parts; while

scattered along the ground were visible the
members from which they had been separated.
And serving as nutriment to the wolf-dogs by
which the savages were accompanied.

The fight at Fort Meigs cemented into history the ignominy
of Dudley's Defeat for the Americans, and the compassion of
Tecumseh. It was a key turning point in the war. The number
of dead was always in dispute, but there was no question the
Americans had been given a severe licking. They had more
than two hundred dead, many dozens wounded, and hundreds
captured. The British-Indian losses were tiny by comparison.

In a way, it was a victory for Harrison. His troops had
been savaged out in the woods, but his fort had held. Once
again the Americans learned that Indians on the loose in the
countryside were hard to beat. They were not nearly as effective
against the gopher game in which their enemy burrowed
inside a fort. Fort Meigs could only be taken in a long siege.
The Indians had no appetite for it and began wandering off
with their bounty. The Canadian militiamen also needed to
go home, to plant their crops before spring became summer.
Procter and Tecumseh had little choice but to end the siege
and return to Amherstburg.

Tecumseh was disappointed. Knocking down Fort Meigs
would have been a keystone in the bridge to regaining all of the
homelands south of Lake Erie. Complete victory would have
been sweet revenge against the hated Harrison, the overseer
of many of Tecumseh's problems. Procter had promised
Tecumseh that after a total Fort Meigs victory, Harrison and
his colleagues who had fought at Tippecanoe would be turned
over to the Shawnee.

The Battle of Fort Meigs created tensions between Tecumseh and General Procter, which grew during the late spring and summer of 1813. Procter was caught between a rock and the proverbial hard place. His priority was to keep his supply lines open back to Niagara, and York. American ships were threatening the supply route out on Lake Erie. The priority for Tecumseh and his warriors remained the land south of Lake Erie, and they argued hard for another attack on Fort Meigs. This was the hard place for Procter: he had to try to keep the Indians happy because without them he could not win his battles.

In June, Amherstburg was the scene of a tense and tough-talking council. When it ended, Procter had very reluctantly agreed to a second attack on Fort Meigs. Between two and three thousand warriors had assembled to fight with Tecumseh. The second battle had little chance of success. Procter was no Isaac Brock. He was prickly and did not have the confidence of all his officers and men, nor was he good at handling his Indian allies. Some military historians believe that Brock would have found a way to compromise between the British and Indian priorities.

The British enthusiasm for the battle was low, and they brought along guns that were smaller than the big shooters that had failed to do the job the first time. The expedition's only hope rested on Tecumseh's plan to draw the Americans out of the fort. General Green Clay commanded the fort while Harrison was travelling farther east with a large body of troops. Tecumseh hoped to stage a ruse in which Clay would send his troops out into the open and Harrison would ride to Fort Meigs in relief.

Tecumseh staged a sham battle to try to trick Clay into believing that Harrison had returned and was being attacked. Clay didn't bite and after a day or two, the second attack on

Fort Meigs was abandoned. A debate began about what to do next. Procter wanted to take troops east toward the Sandusky area where the Indians could purloin some cattle because food supplies were low. Tecumseh protested that he must protect Indian villages in the area against possible American raids. They went their separate ways.

On August 2, Procter attacked Fort Stephenson at Lower Sandusky. It was a disaster. His artillery was too light and he suffered more than one hundred casualties.

It was a shaken and bitter General Procter who returned across the lake to Amherstburg. The decision to attack Fort Stephenson had been unwise, but Procter blamed it on others. His state of mind did not bode well for the important weeks to come.

11

"We Have Met the Enemy..."

As great a commander as he was on land, Tecumseh did not see the big picture of the war the way that Procter did. Procter's command was frontier, isolated from the major centres of Niagara and York, which he had to rely on for supplies and reinforcements. His survival depended on supply lines along the north shore of Lake Erie for food, gunpowder, and reinforcements. If the lines were cut, he could not hope to fight effectively. All that it would take to sever his lines was for an American naval force to sail across Lake Erie, establish a beachhead, and create havoc.

However, the British were superior on the lake. Their lake navy was small and ill-equipped, but still stronger than that of the Americans. The Americans were working like beavers to change that, at a remote and lightly populated outpost on Erie's south shore. It was called Presque Isle, now Erie, Pennsylvania, and in the spring of 1813 a frenzied shipbuilding operation was underway there.

Ordered out from the Atlantic coast to take charge of a desperate attempt to create a little Lake Erie navy was a twenty-seven-year-old Rhode Islander, Master Commandant Oliver Hazard Perry. He struggled through a winter-locked wilderness to get to Presque Isle from the east, and no one would have blamed him if, on his arrival on April Fool's Day 1813, he had dropped to his knees and begun to cry. What he saw was a village of fewer than one hundred houses, many deserted because most of the four hundred residents had abandoned the place on the fear that Canadians and their Indians were going to arrive with tomahawks and scalping knives in hand.

There was sort of a shipyard there with some unfinished vessels sitting up on blocks, but no canvas, no rope, and little wood. Shipwrights, blacksmiths, caulkers, and other shipbuilding trades, all promised to Perry, were not there. There was no sawmill, so lumber for ships had to be cut and squared by hand. Worse, Perry had almost no support from the American navy. His boss, Commodore Isaac Chauncey, was more than 180 miles away at Sackett's Harbour on the east end of Lake Ontario, and had his hands full trying to keep control of that region. Chauncey had commandeered the one hundred and fifty sailors Perry needed to man his new little fleet.

At one point, Perry sent Chauncey a letter of incredible understatement and amazing optimism: "Many are the difficulties we encounter, but we will surmount them all."

Perry was no one's choice for a potential hero. His naval career had been unexceptional, except for three years earlier when his first major command, the fourteen-gun schooner

Revenge, smacked a reef along the New England coast and sank. Perry faced a court martial. He was exonerated but the incident stained his record.

Presque Isle and Perry were an unlikely threat to Procter and Amherstburg — until spring, when Perry somehow overcame huge odds and began building his little fleet. He recruited sailors, trained them, tested his ships, and watched what was happening at Amherstburg closely.

While Perry was building his navy, Tecumseh returned from the second battle of Fort Meigs and settled his people in a new village on Grosse Isle in the Detroit River, across from Amherstburg. He was anxious for the next offensive and brightened when he received word that General Harrison was moving north with a large force. Tecumseh was confident his people and the British could defeat them outside of their forts.

Roundhead, an important Tecumseh ally, reflected the mood of the pro-British-Canadian Indians when he told an August 23 council at Brownstown, on the Michigan side of the Detroit River:

> We are happy to learn Your Father (Harrison) is coming out of his hole, as he has been like a ground hog under the ground and (his advance) will save us much trouble in walking to meet him.

The reference to "Your Father (Harrison)" was directed at some of the Indians who were playing the double-cross game. They had judged that the tide had turned slightly in Harrison's favour and they were considering joining him to be on the winning side.

What Tecumseh and his warriors did not know, and what Procter had not told them, was that the west end of Upper Canada was in peril. The Americans were harassing and threatening supply lines to Amherstburg, and Harrison was just waiting for the British to weaken. Maintaining an adequate line of food and other supplies was leaving Procter's people hungrier than they should have been and short of battle supplies.

Tecumseh got a hint of this late in August when young Perry, his ships built, manned, and out doing mischief, demonstrated off Amherstburg, basically thumbing his nose at the Redcoat navy and daring them to come out and fight. No ships sailed out to take up the dare and Tecumseh demanded to know why. He was told that their big ships were not yet ready.

Some of the warriors believed that the Recoats were afraid to fight but, in fact, their ships were awaiting armaments and other rigging, and were short of men. It was another discouraging sign that the British were not nearly as committed to the cause as the Indians, who now had no confidence in General Procter. Only in General Brock had they found a genuine warrior who did not look for an excuse to back off from battle.

Tecumseh considered leaving the British and going back to his Ohio home. At one point in 1813 he gathered tribal representatives and told them that he planned to quit because the British were always breaking their promises:

> [W]e are treated by them like the dogs of snipe hunters; we are always sent ahead to start the game: it is better that we should return to our country, and let the Americans come on and fight the British.

Some chiefs talked him out of his low moment, and he decided to stay with the British. He knew that only with professional military help could he regain the Ohio homelands.

The Indians saw Procter as a hesitating sissy, but they had respect for the officer who was in charge of the British fleet on Lake Erie. Captain Robert Barclay was certainly no coward. He was a fearless fighter who had lost his left arm to a cannonball while serving with Admiral Nelson at the Battle of Trafalgar. He wanted to fight but needed reinforcements and supplies. His situation was getting desperate, as he noted in a letter to the British naval powers that be:

> The last letter I had the honor of writing to you, dated the 6th instant, I informed you, that unless certain intimation was received of more seamen being on their way to Amherstburg, I should be obliged to sail with the squadron deplorably manned as it was, to fight the enemy (who blockaded the port), to enable us to get supplies of provisions and stores of every description; so perfectly destitute of provisions was the port, that there was not a days flour in store, and the crews of the squadron under my command were on half allowance of many things, and when that was done there was no more.

On September 9, Barclay had some of what he needed but could wait no longer because the Americans had interrupted the supply lines so badly that Amherstburg was going hungry. He suspected that the American fleet was huddled in the Bass

Robert Heriot Barclay, who lost his left arm to a cannonball at the Battle of Trafalgar, fought gallantly but was defeated in the battle of Lake Erie. Tecumseh called him "Our Father with One Arm."

Islands, just thirty-one miles south in the southwest end of Lake Erie. His flagship HMS *Detroit* led HMS *Queen Charlotte*, HMS *Lady Prevost*, HMS *Hunter*, HMS *Little Belt*, and HMS *Chippawa* across the lake to do battle the next day.

At 7:00 a.m., Perry sailed toward the British ships in the USS *Lawrence*, which flew a blue battle flag embroidered with the words Don't Give Up the Ship, the dying words of Captain James Lawrence, killed in a naval battle off Boston three months earlier. Behind him were USS *Niagara*, USS *Ariel*, USS *Caledonia*, USS *Scorpion* , USS *Somers* , USS *Porcupine* , USS *Tigress*, and USS *Trippe*.

Tecumseh was on shore, probably unaware that the outcome of this water battle would change the course of the war. At 11:45 a.m., the roar of the cannons was heard at Amherstburg. Some British positioned themselves on the shore south of Amherstburg to try to view the battle through telescopes. They saw only clouds of cannon smoke. Everyone was on edge, wanting to know the outcome.

Inside the gun smoke, Barclay had a wind advantage and began to give a severe beating to the *Lawrence*, which had found itself alone and far in front of its supporting ships. By 12:15 p.m., Perry was able to lay heavy fire on the British, but his *Lawrence* was overwhelmed with 80 percent casualties. He decided to abandon ship and jumped into a rowboat with four crewmen. As they rowed through smoke and flying lead to the *Niagara*, Perry draped the *Lawrence's* blue battle flag around his shoulders. Safely aboard, he took command and ordered the ship to be sailed boldly into the British fleet with cannons blazing.

By 3:00 p.m. the wind favoured the Americans, and so did the battle. Barclay was wounded, and other senior officers were dead. The British were forced to admit defeat and their captured ships were taken into Put-in-Bay on South Bass Island.

News of the U.S. victory reached General William Harrison in a simple but dramatic message from Perry:

> We have met the enemy and they are ours —
> two ships, two brigs, one schooner and a sloop.

At Amherstburg there were no messages, just silence and dissipating smoke far off on the horizon. Some believed that Barclay had won, but no one knew for sure. Darkness fell, followed by another day of silence with no sails on the horizon. Procter is said to have told Tecumseh that Barclay had won, but that his ships were damaged and he was refitting them at the Bass Islands.

Another day passed in silence and no signal from the lake. Then another. It became apparent that Barclay was defeated and the Americans now controlled Lake Erie and the supply lines for Procter's British-Indian-Canadian army. An invasion and the loss of a large part of Upper Canada to the Americans now appeared inevitable.

No one could blame Barclay. He had fought valiantly and his remaining arm had been torn apart by grape shot, plus his leg was wounded. When the Americans later released him he was court martialled but acquitted of any wrongdoing in the battle. In fact, the court martial praised his courage and ruled that the battle had been lost because he did not have the men and equipment needed to win.

General Harrison was perched across the lake, contemplating how he would swoop down on the western end of Upper Canada. All that stood in the way of his invasion was an exposed and weakened Procter, and of course Tecumseh, who was known for never giving ground easily.

12

Invasion!

The Bass Islands, just off the Marblehead Peninsula near Sandusky, Ohio, had never seen such activity. Boats of different sorts came and went, unloading men and their tents, mess kits, weapons, and food supplies. There was much clatter and clamour as barrels and wooden boxes were stacked atop each other. Five thousand men were bivouacked on the six or seven acres of Middle Bass, where Major-General William Harrison gathered field guns, food, and other provisions. Master Commandant Oliver Perry stood ready with a fleet of ships and boats to transport the men and their battle supplies across the lake to Amherstburg.

When Harrison had received Perry's "We Have Met the Enemy" message he had ordered an immediate, massive movement of troops and supplies to the shore of Lake Erie for transport onto the Bass Islands, then onward to an invasion of

Canada. He had ten thousand fighting men in various camps near the lake, ready to "fight for the rights of their insulted country." Five thousand would make up the invading force, while the rest would be posted at various forts in case Procter and Tecumseh decided to attack first.

Unknown to Tecumseh, Procter not only had no plans for other attacks, but he also planned to run from the impending invasion. Tecumseh learned of Procter's retreat plans on September 14, when a group of angry Indians brought him startling news: they had seen the Redcoats tearing down a wall of Fort Malden at Amherstburg. This could mean only one thing: Procter planned to abandon Amherstburg and not fight the Americans! Tecumseh was not the only one shocked by the news. Some of Procter's own officers did not know of the secret plan to retreat. The Indians camped around Amherstburg were outraged.

Procter's decision, made without consulting his officers or Indian allies, was seen as another link in the long chain of British treachery, including when the Redcoats closed the Fort Miami gates against the desperate Indians back in 1794. The British style, in the view of the Indians, was to promise much and deliver little.

The relationship between Tecumseh and Procter, never friendly, was now hostile. Tecumseh should have been an equal partner in the alliance; he had personally delivered the many hundreds of Indian warriors that the British needed to survive on the Detroit River frontier. Procter did not have anything like Brock's respect for the Indians. Earlier in the summer he referred to Tecumseh, in a written communication, as "the king of the forest," a disdainful reference used when he was forced to give in to one of Tecumseh's demands.

On another occasion, the Fort Malden commissary was low on food and Procter fed salt beef to the British soldiers, but horse meat to the Indians. Tecumseh immediately complained to Procter about the warriors getting lesser food, but Procter had indifferently shrugged off the complaint. Tecumseh touched the hilt of Procter's sword and the handle of his own tomahawk saying, "You are Procter. I am Tecumseh," indicating that if the food injustice was not corrected the affair would be settled by a personal duel. Procter realized his ally was serious and ordered a change in the rations.

The situation at Amherstburg became so tense that warriors openly shouted denunciations against the British. Tecumseh demanded that Procter appear before a council. He had a wampum belt symbolizing the unity between the British and the Indians, and he planned to cut it into pieces and throw it at Procter's feet.

Procter reluctantly appeared before a council at Fort Malden on September 18. Tecumseh stood before the council of Redcoats and Indians with the wampum belt in his hands. John Richardson witnessed the scene and wrote:

> The most prominent feature in the picture, however, was Tecumseh. Habited in a close leather dress, his athletic proportions were admirably delineated, while a large plume of white ostrich feathers, by which he was generally distinguished, over shadowing his brow, and contrasting with the darkness of his complexion and the brilliancy of his black and piercing eye, gave a singularly wild and terrific expression to his features. It was evident that he could be terrible.

Procter told the council that he would destroy the forts and some town buildings at Detroit and Amherstburg, then would retreat up the Thames River to Niagara, to join other British forces. Tecumseh protested abandoning positions without meeting the Americans. In a powerful speech, he accused Procter of cowardice, which he compared to the bravery of Captain Barclay, who now lay wounded among the Americans.

Tecumseh's speech was recorded by an interpreter and was later found among papers left behind by Procter. Interpreters usually were not well-educated but had learned Indian languages, so they were often asked to record on paper what was said at important meetings. The words they recorded were not exactly what an Indian speaker might have said, but they were a reasonable facsimile:

> Listen! When war was declared, our Father stood up and gave us the tomahawk, and told us that he was now ready to strike the Americans that he wanted our assistance; and that he would certainly get us our lands back, which the Americans had taken from us.
>
> Listen! You told us at that time to bring forward our families to this place we did so, and you promised to take care of them, and that they should want for nothing, while the men would go and fight the enemy that we were not to trouble ourselves with the enemy's garrisons that we knew nothing about them, and that our Father would attend to that part of the business. You also told your red children that you would take good care of their garrison here, which made our hearts glad.

Listen! When we last went to the Rapids, it is true we gave you little assistance. It is hard to fight people who live like ground-hogs.

Father, Listen! Our fleet has gone out; we know they have fought; we have heard the great guns; but know nothing of what has happened to our Father with one arm. Our ships have gone one way, and we are much astonished to see our Father tying up everything and preparing to run away … without letting his red children know what his intentions are. You always told us to remain here and take care of our lands; it made our hearts glad to hear that was your wish. Our great Father, the king, is the head, and you represent him. You always told us you would never draw your foot off British ground; but now, Father, we see you are drawing back, and we are sorry to see our Father doing so without seeing the enemy. We must compare our Father's conduct to a fat animal, that carries its tail upon its back, but when affrighted, it drops it between its legs and runs off.

Father! You have got the arms and ammunition which our great Father sent for his red children. If you have any idea of going away, give them to us, and you may go in welcome, for us. Our lives are in the hands of the Great Spirit. We are determined to defend our lands, and if it is his will, we wish to leave our bones upon them.

The talk of dying for their lands sent the Indians to their feet, shouting and waving their tomahawks.

Procter then admitted that Barclay was defeated on the lake. He said he would consider what he had heard and attend another council in two days. Just before that council, Procter met Tecumseh and explained the seriousness of Barclay's defeat. A compromise was reached: the retreat would be to the forks of the Thames River at Chatham village, and there they would make a stand.

On a fine autumn morning a week later, sixteen armed vessels and one hundred boats filled with American soldiers sailed a light breeze out of the Bass Islands, and set a course for the Canadian shore. In each vessel, General Harrison's orders to the troops were read:

> The general entreats his brave troops to remember that they are the sons of sires whose fame is immortal; that they are to fight for the rights of their insulted country, while their opponents combat for the unjust pretensions of a master. Kentuckians! Remember the River Raisin! but remember it only while victory is suspended. The revenge of a soldier cannot be gratified upon a fallen enemy.

Shouts of "Harrison and Victory!" rose from the boats.

The flotilla hit the sandy shores at Hartley's Point, about four miles south of Amherstburg, late in the afternoon. The landing spot featured sand dunes, behind which the enemy was expected to be hiding. There was no resistance to the landing and the troops marched toward Amherstburg, confronted only by townswomen pleading with the Americans to do no harm. The marching song

Yankee Doodle mingled in the autumn air with clouds of smoke coming from the dockyard, some public buildings, and the remains of Fort Malden as the troops entered town.

From a distance, two men on horseback listened to the pipes and drums, and watched the invaders arrive. One was Tecumseh, the other Captain Matthew Elliott, soldier, politician, and former Indian agent. Both were sickened by the Americans' return to Canadian soil. Certainly for Tecumseh, the scene was part of a nightmare in which he never again sees his homeland below Lake Erie.

The British rear guard was only one hour down the road when the Americans arrived. Its job was to burn the bridge over the Canard River to block the American advance, but Procter's retreat plan couldn't even get that right. American cavalry arrived as the fire was set; a few shots chased the British away, and the bridge was saved. The next morning the invaders tramped across it en route to Sandwich, where they would join Perry's naval forces and the main cavalry force travelling by land.

After watching the Americans enter Amherstburg, Tecumseh rode to Sandwich where Redcoats and militia were beginning the retreat along the shore of Lake St. Clair to the mouth of the Thames River. The retreat road led through the village of Chatham and on to London. He met Indians who refused to join the retreat. Their collective spirit was sagging and they were uncertain who would win this time. They wanted to be on the winning side because it was the difference between being fed and going hungry. They were pawns manipulated by battling kings.

The Indian warriors were not like the white soldiers, who had only themselves and their comrades to look after. The warriors brought not just their support to the British, they brought their villages of women, children, and the elderly. Moving was part of the Indian way of life, but it was brutally difficult during war. The women bore the burdens of packing food, utensils, and clothing. They were the ones who still had to ensure that there was food, fire to cook it with, shelter for the nights, medicine for the sick and wounded, and care for those who could not move quickly on their own. Warriors might talk of brave deeds, but the heroes of these wars were truly the women, like Tecumseh's elder sister Tecumapease, who was a maternal chief among the Shawnee at their Grosse Isle village. She and the other women were responsible for moving the village to wherever the fighting men required it.

Food was a critical issue, and a prime reason why Procter wanted to retreat. Besides his troops and some Canadian militia, he also had to feed his Indian allies. There simply was not enough forest food to feed roughly three thousand people, each of whom might consume one pound of meat a day. A twelve-hundred-pound steer was good for roughly 570 pounds of butchered meat. Doing the math, that was three thousand people consuming 3,300 pounds of meat, or roughly five steers every day. That was a big order, even before the Americans severed Procter's supply lines.

On October 1, Tecumseh was one of the last to leave Sandwich and reach the mouth of the Thames River. There he met more warriors coming back; they were deserting the alliance. Tecumseh found that almost half of his three thousand supporters had drifted away. He pushed on and arrived at Chatham village the next day to find the British camped on one side of the river and his Indians on the other, the side on which the Americans would come. There was no sign of Procter, no fortifications, no evidence that this was where they would fight the Americans as promised. All that was there was a house filled with small arms and a few dismantled cannons scattered on the ground.

Tecumseh exploded. Another broken promise! The Indians were in an uproar. Scouts had spotted Harrison's army only four or five miles behind. When Tecumseh demanded that the British cross the river to join and support him they refused, saying they had no boats. Then he received a message from Procter, who had kept far ahead of the troops, saying he had found a good defensive spot near Moraviantown, and that was where they would make their stand against Harrison.

Moraviantown was a village along the Thames River trail, roughly twenty miles east of Chatham. There the Moravian Church, which had grown out of protests against the Roman Catholic Church in Czechoslovakia in the 1400s, had an Indian mission.

The British packed up and marched toward Moraviantown, but Tecumseh still had his women, children, and elderly to worry about. Some were sick and exhausted from the rugged travel. Tecumseh organized them and remained behind with some warriors to slow the Americans, who had started the chase up the Thames two days earlier and were closing fast because the bridges over numerous streams running into Lake St. Clair had been left intact. Apparently, Procter had not anticipated that Harrison's army would pursue him by land.

Master Commandant Perry brought some boats up the Thames to where the water narrowed and quickened. He couldn't navigate farther so the rest of the chase would be by land. So high was the excitement that Perry, a sea fighter, decided to be part of the land battle and joined Harrison as a volunteer aide.

There were two bridges at McGregor's Creek, which joined the Thames at Chatham. Tecumseh's warriors burnt one bridge upstream, but a large one at the mouth of the creek was too wet so its planks were lifted, leaving the beams only. They hid in the underbrush near the creek and waited for the Americans.

Harrison had three thousand men marching along the Thames, including one thousand mounted Kentucky volunteers led by their aging state governor, Isaac Shelby, and the dashing Colonel Richard Mentor Johnson. Tecumseh had no hope of stopping them at the creek; he could only slow their advance. Tecumseh's men opened fire when the Americans approached. Harrison turned two six-pound cannons on their position, plus volleys of musket balls, one of which hit Tecumseh in the arm. There was no hope of making a stand against the punishing fire. Tecumseh ordered guns and munitions left by the British burned, and retreated toward Moraviantown.

Harrison's men repaired the bridge and extinguished the fire in the house containing the small arms. The arms left behind by Procter that Tecumseh had tried to burn in a hurry, were more evidence that Procter's retreat was a rout. Boats, barges, deserters, and supplies were taken by Harrison's troops as they advanced up the Thames. All this pointed to a disorderly retreat, rather than a well thought out defensive strategy.

The British were in no mood for a fight. They were exhausted and weak from hunger. They would have rather kept giving up ground to get safely to Niagara. For Tecumseh, every inch given up took him farther from Ohio and the dream of regaining the homelands. He arrived at the encampments just below Moraviantown in the evening. There are plenty of stories of how Tecumseh spent that evening. Some historians report that other Indians found him reflective, knowing that his cause was lost. Romanced accounts say he reminisced with followers and predicted his death on the following day.

Certainly he realized that the odds were against him when the Americans arrived. He had only five hundred warriors still with him, perhaps eight hundred hungry, weak, and dispirited Redcoats, and a general who would rather not fight. That was more than enough reason to be reflective.

13

"The Forlorn Hope"

Procter found his good defensive position at Moraviantown, but failed to use it. When he had gone ahead to find it, he had taken most of his artillery, some ammunition, and cooking utensils. When the troops awakened the morning of October 5, to resume their march, they had nothing to cook with and were reduced to meagre rations. This, combined with fatigue and the confusion of what exactly was planned, sunk them deeper into misery.

They resumed marching and about two and a half miles below Moraviantown were joined by their general, who halted the march and formed the troops up along the wagon path on the north bank of the Thames. Procter apparently believed that Harrison was immediately on his tail. He was very close to his Moraviantown defensive site, but decided he must fight there without his cannons, except for one six-pounder.

The Americans were close behind, but not as close as Procter believed. As the day progressed, Colonel Johnson and some men galloped forward to gain intelligence, and captured a British waggoner who told them that Procter had positioned his troops on the roadway very close by. Johnson crept forward and saw the British setting up in battle order. He took note of the setup and reported back to Harrison and a council of officers.

Johnson realized the spot chosen by Procter to make a stand was not a bad one. To the left of the British was the Thames River, which at this point was fairly placid below its high banks. To the right was a marsh running parallel to the river. Roughly three hundred feet from the river, and between it and the marsh, was a small swamp. The middle ground, over which the wagon track ran, was hardwood forest with large beeches, oaks, and sugar maples and only moderate undergrowth.

Procter had positioned the six-pound cannon on the wagon track and had formed up his regulars in two lines between the small swamp and the river. From the edge of the small swamp to the marsh were Tecumseh, other war chiefs, and their warriors, sort of hidden where the underbrush was a bit thicker. The idea was to drive the Americans against the river, with the Indians blocking their left flank and the six-pounder forcing them off the wagon path. The Indian women, children, and elderly were secured off in the distance near Moraviantown.

When the battle was imminent, Tecumseh visited the British lines to offer the men encouragement and good luck. Richardson described it:

> Only a few minutes before the clang of the
> American bugles was heard ringing through
> the forest, and inspiriting to action, the haughty

Chieftain had passed along our line, pleased with the manner in which his left was supported, and seemingly sanguine of success. He was dressed in his usual deer skin dress, which admirably displayed his right yet sinewy figure, and in his handkerchief, rolled as a turban over his brow, was placed a handsome white ostrich feather, which had been given to him by a near relation of the writer of this narrative, and on which he was ever fond of decorating himself, either for the Hall of Council or the battle field. He pressed the hand of each officer as he passed, made some remark in Shawnee, appropriate to the occasion, which was sufficiently understood by the expressive signs accompanying them, and then passed away forever from our view.

There is a story that Tecumseh unbuckled his sword and, placing it in the hands of one of his fellow warriors, said, "When my son becomes a noted warrior, and able to wield a sword, give this to him." It is possible that this did happen, but there is no irrefutable evidence that it ever did. His son Paukeesau was with Tecumseh at the battle ground. He was seventeen, certainly the age when he was "able to wield a sword," unless this was a reference to what some historians have referred to as Tecumseh's disdain for the young man because he was not the warrior type. However, Paukeesau was at the battle and did carry a musket because Captain William Caldwell, a well-known Loyalist and partner of Matthew Elliott, fought that day and recalled meeting Paukeesau as they retreated.

By mid-afternoon, Harrison's full force of three thousand-plus men was upon them. Harrison had only 120 U.S.-Army regulars, but 2,380 militia, and 260 Indians. At the head of these were one thousand Kentucky cavalry, burning with hatred for the British and their Indian allies, and seeking revenge for the River Raisin massacre and other defeats. Procter had an estimated eight hundred Redcoats mixed with Canadian militia, and perhaps five hundred natives under Tecumseh.

Harrison planned to make simultaneous cavalry charges: one led by Colonel Johnson into the Indians, the other into the British lines by Johnson's brother, James. Once they broke through the lines, they would turn and attack again from the rear. A bugle sounded and the word "Charge!" floated through the trees. Galloping horsemen followed volleys of musket fire into the British lines.

Within minutes, James Johnson's Kentuckians had dozens of Redcoats scattered across the ground. The rest of the British surrendered or fled. Procter's six-pound cannon never fired a shot. For the British, the battle was over, and Procter was seen galloping off toward Moraviantown, where some of his troops were still preparing his defences. One version of the battle has him stopping only briefly at the village, then galloping off farther east. Once again, Tecumseh and his Indians had been abandoned, left to deal with an overwhelming enemy force.

Colonel Johnson had a tougher assignment because the Indians were in the soft terrain at the swamp's edge where horses would have difficulty. Johnson charged with twenty American cavalrymen dubbed "The Forlorn Hope" because they would ride directly into the Indians' musket fire and flying tomahawks. An officer with Johnson wrote about the charge years after the battle:

> I was at the head or right of my company, on horseback, waiting orders, at about fifty or

sixty yards from the line of the enemy. Colonel
Johnson rode up and explained to me the mode
of attack ... In a few minutes the trumpet
sounded, and the word "charge'" was given by
Colonel Johnson. The colonel charged within
a few paces of me. We struck the Indian line
obliquely, and when we approached within ten
or fifteen yards of their line, the Indians poured
in a heavy fire upon us, killing ten or fifteen
of our men and several horses, and wounded
Colonel Johnson very severely.

Johnson's charge indeed lived up to the name Forlorn Hope
in the first few minutes. Horses screamed above the battle din as
they fell, struck by musket balls or toppled by the uneven ground.
The bitter smoke of black powder filled the forest as Kentuckian
after Kentuckian fell into the dirt as Tecumseh's warriors cut
them down. More than a dozen died in the first firings. Others
scrambled off their horses to engage in close order firing, and
hand-to-hand combat.

Colonel Johnson was hit once, then twice and twice more
by musket balls, but stayed in the saddle. For a brief time it
appeared the Indians would carry at least this part of the battle.
What happened next is the most contested point in the Battle
of the Thames.

Johnson reeled in his saddle, on the verge of dropping off,
when he was spotted by Tecumseh, who was battling fiercely
and was wounded. The Shawnee chief charged forward,
tomahawk raised high and ready to be whirled into Johnson's
head. The colonel was hardly lucid but had a pistol in one
hand. Before the tomahawk flew he fired it into Tecumseh's

The Battle of the Thames and the death of Tecumseh as depicted in this engraving by John Dorival, 1833, shows Richard Mentor Johnson as the slayer of the great Shawnee chief.

chest. The tomahawk fell harmlessly to the earth and behind it, Tecumseh.

There is much dispute over whether the Indian shot was Tecumseh, or if Johnson fired the shot that felled him. Johnson himself was in no shape to identify the attacker and simply said for years afterward that if people on the field said it had been his shot that had killed Tecumseh, then he guessed it had been. Certainly public belief that he killed Tecumseh, America's great enemy, propelled him to great political heights later.

Whatever the exact details, word spread rapidly of Tecumseh's fall, sucking the fight from the Indians like a giant vacuum. They fell back, dispirited, and the Battle of the Thames ended as an overwhelming American victory. Procter's side suffered 155 dead or wounded, and 477 captured. Tecumseh's force lost thirty-three. The Americans had fifteen killed and thirty wounded — most of the casualties coming from the charge on the Indians.

Just before dusk fell that night, the Americans walked the small battlefield collecting and tending to the wounded and identifying the dead. Anthony Shane, a mixed blood who had known Tecumseh most of his life, identified the Shawnee chief's body, as did some captured British officers later. The body had a musket ball hole over the heart, some buckshot wounds, and a cut on the head. The Kentuckians mutilated the body, scalping it and taking strips of skin for prized razor strops.

There are different accounts of what happened after Tecumseh fell. One says his body was spirited off for secret burial before the Kentuckians got to it. Another says it was weighted down with stones in the Thames River. Another says the body was buried, but later exhumed and taken to Walpole Island in the St. Clair River.

Whatever happened to the actual body didn't change the fact that Tecumseh, probably the most important native Indian in North American history, was gone. And gone with him was the dream of restoring the native way of life that had existed for centuries before the coming of the Europeans.

Epilogue

The Americans won the Battle of the Thames, but the victory little changed the overall war. It continued back and forth for another year, with little resolved. During the course of the war the Americans burned York (Toronto), the Upper Canada capital, and the British burned Washington. The two sides agreed to call it quits late in 1814, leaving the boundaries between the new United States of America and Canada much as they had been before the war had started.

As in every war, the big losers were the family and friends of the sixteen hundred British and 2,260 American soldiers killed in battle, not including the roughly eight thousand total wounded, and the many hundreds of Indians and militiamen on both sides.

Harrison achieved his goal: to deal a knockout blow to the Indian resistance to American settlement in the Old Northwest.

He had little interest in that small and isolated piece of Upper Canada bordering the Detroit River, so he withdrew home.

For the Indians, the Battle of the Thames was not just another battle lost. Gone forever was Tecumseh's dream: re-establishment of the Ohio frontier below Lake Erie as a Native American homeland. There would be other Indian uprisings as settlement advanced farther south and west: Creeks waged war in the southeast, but were crushed; various tribes including the Apache, Sioux, and Navajo fought the American advance well into the 1800s. But there was no stopping a lust for land that left no room for Native Americans.

Tecumseh and other great chiefs, such as Pontiac and Joseph Brant, had tried to hold back the powerful tide of settlement, but they had been set up to fail before they even started. Uniting the Indians was an impossible task. The Europeans saw them as people without organized government who managed their affairs in chaos. In fact, the Indians had a system of government that was pinned solidly to a search for consensus. Indian peoples talked things out extensively to reach consensus. When consensus could not be reached, minorities who did not agree with the majorities simply walked away along their own path.

This system made it difficult to bring Indians together. Indian nations did not always agree, neither did divisions or tribes within nations, nor groups or clans within tribes. Various components of Indian society were free to follow their own trails in life. This is why Indians from the same nations fought against each other after choosing to join the British or American sides. The only hope they had against the Europeans were great leaders who had the stature, respect, and eloquence to convince independent nations and tribes that their real power existed in a confederacy or pan-Indian movement. Tecumseh was the greatest — and last — hope for such a confederacy.

The Ottawa chief Naywash lamented the passing of the great chief and the idea of confederacy soon after the Battle of the Thames:

> Since our great chief Tecumtha has been killed, we do not listen to one another, we do not rise together, we hurt ourselves by it. It is our own fault, it is not our Father's fault.
>
> You warriors, when our Father gives us good encouragement, we hurt ourselves, we do not, when we go to war, rise together, but we go one or two and the rest say they will go tomorrow.

Not much more than a week following the battle, some tribes who were involved in the fight signed a truce with the Americans. Harrison met with various Indian groups outlining his conditions for peace, but there were no immediate demands for land cessions. Those came later, and Indians were systematically removed from Ohio, then Indiana, Illinois, and Michigan.

General Henry Procter's retreat from Amherstburg was not viewed kindly by his bosses. The British court-martialled him on five charges: he did not begin his retreat soon enough; he slowed the retreat by taking too much baggage, some of it personal; he did not take care to ensure supplies and ammunition did not fall into American hands; he neglected to properly fortify his position along the Thames; and he failed to rally and encourage his troops and Indian allies.

The outcome of the court martial was a bit of a dog's breakfast. Procter was found innocent of the first charge and partially guilty on the others. The end result was that the military judges found in him "deficien[t] in energy and judgment." He was suspended for six months without pay, but his sentence was later reduced to a reprimand. He was finished in the military and would go down in history as an indecisive and ineffective leader, if not an outright coward.

Historians have speculated on what the outcome might have been had Procter been Brock. But he wasn't Brock. He was a man lacking the fire in the gut that marks outstanding leaders like Brock, Tecumseh, and Harrison.

Harrison and Colonel Johnson soared to even greater heights following their victory. Johnson was a Congressman before the War of 1812–14 and resumed his political career in the spring of 1814, when he returned to Congress a war hero — the man who killed the great Tecumseh. He was elected the country's ninth vice-president in 1836, as the running mate for President Martin Van Buren. He and Van Buren sought re-election in 1840, in a hard-fought campaign. Johnson gave speeches recalling the fight along the Thames, and in one campaign stop opened his shirt to show everyone his battle scars. However, the Van Buren-Johnson ticket lost the 1840 election to the other hero of the Thames, William Henry Harrison, who became the ninth president of the United States.

Harrison, now nicknamed Old Tippecanoe, or Old Tip, campaigned as a simple frontier Indian fighter, ignoring the fact that he was born to the Virginia aristocracy. He delivered his inaugural speech on a cold day in March 1840, without wearing a hat or coat. He caught a cold that turned to pneumonia and he died after only thirty-one days in office. His death started the extraordinary string of coincidences that become known as Tecumseh's Curse, in which every president elected in a year ending in zero died before finishing his term. About the same time that Harrison was dying, the British invited Tecumapease and Paukeesau to Quebec City, as guests of Sir George Prevost, governor of colonial Canada. Tenskwatawa the Prophet was not invited because the British, and many Indians, considered him a charlatan.

The British hospitality and presents could not lift the sadness of Tecumseh's relatives. Tecumapease lost both her brother and her husband, Wahsikegaboe, at the Thames. They received some kind words from Sir George and Lady Prevost. Said Sir George:

> Our Great Father considers you as his children
> and will not forget you or your interests.…

It was typical talk from the British, who had no true understanding of the Indian cause and Indian suffering. The British saw them as unfortunate children whose future lay in adopting British ways, culture, and religion.

Tecumapease returned to the frontier, likely at or near Detroit, which was back in U.S. hands and where Indians who had once allied with the British were being repatriated. She is believed to have died there in her early fifties.

Paukeesau returned to Ohio, and became a Shawnee civil chief, an authority he later surrendered to someone else. He went on to live in obscurity west of the Mississippi, and is not known to have distinguished himself in any way. The British awarded him an annual pension as part of their wish to look after their important ally's family. He died out West in about 1843.

The position of Shawnee war chief fell to Tenskwatawa, even though he had never participated in a battle. He was at Moraviantown, but had stayed well out of the action. He lived at

Amherstburg for a while, trying in vain to rally support for his cause, but mainly bothering the British for supplies, including rum. He returned to his old self, turning to alcohol again, but still hearing the voice of the Great Spirit, and still professing that Indians should return to the old ways. He too moved west of the Mississippi, and died in 1836.

For the Indians, the rest is history, as they say. Almost two hundred years after Tecumseh's fight to preserve Indian life, Canadian First Nations living conditions are ranked No. 63, or at Third World level, based on the United Nations human development index. First Nations people in Canada have an infant mortality rate 1.5 times higher than the rest of Canadians, their average life span is roughly six years shorter, and they are imprisoned at a greater rate than other Canadians. In general, compared to other Canadians, Canada's First Nations people are less educated, sicker, have double the national unemployment rate, have fewer opportunities, and live in substandard housing. As of May 2003, at least one hundred First Nations communities had to boil water before using it.

Similar conditions exist for native people in the United States; however, Americans retain a powerful admiration for Tecumseh and his efforts to improve the lot of Indians.

Tecumseh is an honoured name in the United States, which seems odd considering that many of the Americans of his time considered him a terrorist. His battles against American settlement expansion were considered savage and hateful. His siding with the British in the War of 1812 made him an enemy many times over. His message that the land was the common property of all tribes irritated the Americans, who saw land as a commodity to be sliced and diced and sold, in a relentless march toward more prosperity.

Yet, after the Battle of the Thames, Americans elevated Tecumseh to honoured spots, naming towns, buildings, warships, machinery, and monuments after him. William Tecumseh Sherman, the famous U.S. Civil War general, was one of many Americans named for him. Sherman's father, Judge Charles Sherman, took some heat from friends and neighbours for naming a son after a "savage," but always replied that Tecumseh was "a great warrior." General Sherman, called "Cump" as a boy, was born in Lancaster, Ohio, not far from the Shawnee centre of Old Chillicothe.

The story of Tecumseh holds valuable lessons for those of us living today, even though his time was two hundred years ago and much different.

One lesson is the importance of viewing situations from more than one perspective. To the struggling young country of the United States, Tecumseh was a dangerous terrorist bent on blocking the American Dream. He and his people fought viciously to stop expanding settlement that the Americans saw as a good thing for everyone. More settlement meant growth, prosperity, and better living conditions in a rich and vibrant new land.

Tecumseh's perspective was very different, but just as valid. He saw his way of life being destroyed by people who came from afar, people who could not or would not understand his point of view. To him, more settlement meant more people who could not be sustained by the natural resources needed by the Indians to live. He and his people had most everything they needed or wanted and could not understand why anyone needed more.

Today, we expect such conflicts might be settled, or at least reduced, by studying the perspectives of different sides and trying to develop compromise.

The American lust for land was not just a North American Native complaint. Others, with original European backgrounds, believed the new American state was too aggressive in pushing the Indians off their lands. For instance, Robert Hamilton, Niagara-area businessman and politician, noted in a 1792 letter to John Graves Simcoe, Upper Canada lieutenant-governor:

> The Americans seem possessed with a species of mania for getting lands which has no bounds. Their Congress, prudent, reasonable and wise in other matters, in this seems as much infected as the people.

Tecumseh, with no education and little outside contact, was able to grasp a concept expressed long before his time by English poet John Donne. Donne wrote that "no man is an island, entire of itself...." Tecumseh grasped that a united Indian front was critical to stopping land losses and saving the Indian ways of life. He knew that Indian resistance was not enough to achieve what he wanted. He needed to change Indian thinking from a tribal perspective to a common front, supported by a wide variety of Indian nations and tribes.

Tecumseh was a champion, but a failed one. However, his story shows that you don't always have to be an outstanding success to achieve. Tecumseh's belief in Indian traditions and land rights was rock solid, important enough to fight and die for. Everyone needs to believe in something and to be willing to stand up for it. However, Tecumseh was not unreasonable in defending his beliefs. He did try oratory and compromise and other means besides violence. Many other Indian leaders simply caved in and abandoned their beliefs, while still others would not consider any approach other than war.

Savagery is something expected from warlike men such as Tecumseh. He was among the most feared people in battle, yet there is no evidence that he was vicious, or even mean-spirited. He was courageous and also honourable, compassionate and magnanimous. He had a sense of who he was and how he should behave without being unduly influenced by others. His compassionate treatment of prisoners and the sick, elderly, and less fortunate of his own tribe is well-documented. He also was industrious and active, always in motion.

The most powerful evidence of those character traits is found in the respect he received among his enemies. Harrison, noting that "No difficulties deterred him," called the obedience and respect paid to Tecumseh by his followers truly "astonishing." Other important enemies had similar praise for Tecumseh, but nothing speaks more about respect for him than American tributes to his memory at two of that country's most important sites.

The U.S. Naval Academy at Annapolis, Maryland, has a bronze statue named Tecumseh. It is a replica of an Indian figurehead taken from the U.S.S. *Delaware*, which was sunk during the U.S. Civil War. The figurehead was originally named after Delaware Chief Tamanend, but was later renamed Tecumseh to honour the great Shawnee warrior. Midshipmen there offer prayers and pennies to the statue in hope that it will bring them good luck in exams and sporting contests. Tecumseh is given a coat of "war paint" for special occasions, such as Parents' Weekend, Homecoming, before Army-Navy contests, and Commissioning Week.

The most famous tribute is in the Rotunda of the U.S. Capitol Building in Washington, D.C. The Rotunda is the tallest part of the Capitol, considered the symbolic and physical heart

*A stone tablet marks the spot where Tecumseh fell during the
Battle of the Thames, also known as the Battle of Moraviantown.*

of the building. Atop the walls of the Capitol, and just below its
dome windows, is a belt of recessed space on which are painted
nineteen scenes depicting the history of the United States. One
of the scenes in this "Frieze of American History" is "The Death
of Tecumseh," depicting the Battle of the Thames in which a man
on horseback has fired a shot into the chest of the chief.

Physical tributes to Tecumseh in Canada are far less evident.
A few municipal areas are named for him. There is a parkette
with monument to him at the battle site beside the Thames River,

but it is sometimes strewn with garbage and is in need of repair. Southwestern Ontario history buffs are hoping to have a more significant tribute erected for the two hundredth anniversary of his death in 2013.

Tecumseh was not a great Canadian patriot, as some people believe. He had a brief but important role in stopping an American takeover of Canada in the War of 1812–14. But his battles on Canadian soil had nothing to do with wanting to save Canada. His dream was to create a pan-Indian movement that would regain his homelands south of Lake Erie.

His months of fighting alongside the British in Canada were to support his dream. They were of value to Canada. The taking of Detroit by Tecumseh and Brock was a shock to the Americans, who were confident that the War of 1812 would be a cakewalk in which the Canadians would simply lay down their arms. Tecumseh's victories helped build confidence and stiffen Canadian spines, which Brock had noted were somewhat lacking.

A perfectly true picture of Tecumseh is now obscured by time and myths. Through the blur, however, one thing is clear: the man possessed the character traits of strong and dedicated leadership, so often needed and so often lacking both then and now.

Chronology of Tecumseh

Tecumseh and His Times	Canada and the World
1630s–60s Iroquois gain dominance during the Beaver Wars and displace Shawnee from their Ohio River homelands.	
	1669 French explorer Robert de La Salle travels Ohio River Valley country south of Lake Erie and claims the entire region for France.
	1670 May 7: Company of Adventurers of England Trading into Hudson's Bay (Hudson's Bay Company) founded.

Tecumseh and His Times	*Canada and the World*
	1709 Slavery becomes illegal in New France.
	1713 Acadia, Newfoundland, Hudson Bay, and the "Iroquois country" ceded to Britain in the Treaty of Utrecht.
	1744 March 15: France declares war on England.
	1749 Halifax founded to establish strong British foothold in Nova Scotia.
1750s Shawnee begin reunification in the Ohio Country.	
	1754 French and Indian War begins in North America between France, England, and each country's Indian allies.

Tecumseh and His Times	*Canada and the World*
	1755 July: Acadians who refuse to sign oath of allegiance expelled from Nova Scotia.
	1758 October 2: Nova Scotia legislative assembly convenes as the first legislative assembly in British North America with an elected House.
1759 Pukeshinwau and Methoataaskee settle in Ohio River Valley, old homeland of the Shawnee.	**1759** British defeat French on the Plains of Abraham.
1761 Cheeseekau, Tecumseh's eldest sibling, born to Pukeshinwau and Methoataaskee.	
1763 May: Ottawa chief Pontiac leads an uprising against British settlement in the Great Lakes region. His confederacy of Indians will	**1763** France cedes Canada and much of the territory below Lake Erie to Britain, in the Treaty of Paris.

Tecumseh and His Times	*Canada and the World*
be an example for Tecumseh.	October: Britain passes a Royal Proclamation closing all Indian territories west of the Appalachians to colonists, in an effort to contain revolution efforts.

1768
March: Tecumseh born. Iroquois sell parts of Ohio Country to the Thirteen Colonies looking for more land for settlement.

1769
Chief Pontiac murdered in Illinois by another Indian.

1769
October 6: Isaac Brock, later British general and administrator of Upper Canada, is born.

1770
March 5: Five civilians killed by British troops in riot that becomes known as The Boston Massacre.

July: Samuel Hearne's Chipewyan guides massacre Inuit during exploration of the Arctic.

Tecumseh and His Times

1771
Tecumseh's brother
Lalawéthika (Tenskwatawa/
the Prophet) is born.

1774
October 10: Tecumseh's
father, Pukeshinwau, killed at
Battle of Point Pleasant where
Shawnee fight to hold back
American land expansion.

1777
Shawnee move west of
the Scioto River to escape
American infringement.

Canada and the World

1771
July: Explorer Hearne reaches
the Arctic Ocean via the
Coppermine River.

1775
April 19: First shot fired in the
American Revolution.

June 9: Martial law declared
in Canada because of the
American Revolution.

1776
July 4: United States
Declaration of Independence
signed.

Tecumseh and His Times	*Canada and the World*
	1778 Captain James Cook explores Canada's west coast.
1780 August 8: Kentuckians raid Tecumseh's village on the Mad River.	**1780** Beginning of the Underground Railway to transport black slaves from the United States to freedom in Canada.
	1783 September 3: American Revolution ends. British cede all claims to the Ohio Territory to the new United States of America. North West Company formed to compete with Hudson's Bay Company in the fur trade.
	1784 United Empire Loyalists move to Canada from the new United States of America.
1787 Settlers stream West over the Appalachians when U.S. creates the Northwest Territory	

Tecumseh and His Times

Canada and the World

of lands that eventually will become Ohio, Illinois, Indiana, Michigan, Wisconsin, and an edge of Minnesota.

1786–88
Teenager Tecumseh joins brother Cheeseekau and other Shawnee warriors in raids against encroaching American settlers.

1788
Tecumseh and brother Cheeseekau leave for Missouri, but quickly abandon plans to live there.

1789
July 14: French Revolution begins with the storming of the Bastille.

1790
The brothers join the Chickamauga in the raids against settlements along the Tennessee River.
President George Washington

Tecumseh and His Times	*Canada and the World*

Tecumseh and His Times

orders a major offensive to
end the Indian uprisings,
slowing settlement along the
Ohio River.

October: Troops under the
command of General Josiah
Harmar badly mauled by
Indians along the Ohio-
Indiana border.

1791
November 4: Large part of the
army commanded by General
Arthur St. Clair wiped out by
chiefs Blue Jacket and Little
Turtle at the Battle of the
Wabash River.

1792
President Washington, alarmed
by the Indian victories,
establishes the Legion of the
United States, the beginnings
of a professional U.S. army.

June 26: Cheeseekau's
warriors burn Ziegler's Station
(now Nashville), taking

Canada and the World

1791
Constitutional Act creates
Upper and Lower Canada.

1792
August: First Parliament of
Upper Canada elected.

December 20: Fortnightly
mail exchange established
between U.S. and Canada.

Tecumseh and His Times	*Canada and the World*
women and children hostages. The hostages are later sold.	
September: Cheeseekau urges chiefs at Chattanooga to engage in all-out war against American settlement.	
September 30: Cheeseekau killed at raid on Buchanan's Station, Tennessee.	
December: Tecumseh believed to be the leader of warriors who drive off a much larger group of American attackers.	
	1793 July 21: Alexander Mackenzie reaches the Pacific Coast.
1794 August 20: Tecumseh leads a band of Shawnee as part of the Battle of Fallen Timbers near Maumee, Ohio, a battle overwhelmingly won by General (Mad) Anthony Wayne and his new Legion of	**1794** Jay Treaty establishes commission to settle U.S.-Canada border disputes and guarantee Indians free movement across the border.

Tecumseh and His Times	*Canada and the World*

the United States.
After the battle, Tecumseh
leaves the war trail to try to live
a traditional native life away
from American encroachment.

1798
David Thompson, considered
Canada's greatest explorer,
charts the headwaters of the
Mississippi River.

1799
Summer: Tecumseh emerges
from self-imposed exile
to speak to an American
settlement about false rumours
of a new Indian uprising.

1801
Birth of Shanawdithit, who
becomes the last known
survivor of the Beothuks.

1802–05
William Henry Harrison, an
army officer at Fallen Timbers
and new governor of Indiana
Territory, concludes seven

Tecumseh and His Times	*Canada and the World*
treaties, gaining huge pieces of what will become the states of Wisconsin, Indiana, Missouri, and Illinois.	
1803	**1803**
Ohio becomes a state. Tecumseh emerges from obscurity once again to speak to settlers who fear more uprisings.	United States negotiates the Louisiana Purchase, obtaining all lands from west of the Mississippi to the Rockies and from the Gulf of Mexico to Canada. August: Lewis and Clark begin organizing expedition to explore the new U.S. lands to find water routes to the Pacific Ocean.
1805	**1805**
Lalawéthika has a vision and becomes Tenskwatawa, the Prophet.	Lord Nelson of Britain defeats French-Spanish fleets at the Battle of Trafalgar.
1806	**1806**
June 16: An eclipse of the sun, predicted by Tenskwatawa, leads thousands of Indians to believe he is a messenger	John Graves Simcoe, first lieutenant-governor of Upper Canada, dies.

Tecumseh and His Times	*Canada and the World*
from Waashaa Monetoo, the Great Spirit.	

1807

Growth of the Prophet's religious movement alarms white citizenry and American leaders.

Autumn: Tecumseh makes a long speech at Chillicothe, the new Ohio capital, calling for a strong Indian confederacy to defend native land rights.

1808

Tecumseh and Tenskwatawa establish Prophetstown, near the junction of the Wabash and Tippecanoe rivers.

1809

September 10: Harrison concludes the Treaty of Fort Wayne, taking 4,600 square miles of land from the Indians, which convinces Tecumseh to return to the warpath.

1807

November 24: Mohawk Chief Joseph Brant (Thayendanegea), whose followers fought with the British in the American Revolution, dies.

Tecumseh and His Times	*Canada and the World*
1810	
August 12: Historic meeting between Harrison and Tecumseh at Vincennes, Indiana Territory, to discuss American expansion across Indian lands.	
1811	**1811**
July: Tecumseh meets Harrison again at Vincennes. After the meeting, Tecumseh travels extensively to recruit other trines to his confederacy.	November 11: United States' war congress convenes.
	July 15: David Thompson reaches the mouth of the Columbia River in what becomes Washington State.
November 7: Harrison's army takes advantage of Tecumseh's absence to destroy Prophetstown, in the Battle of Tippecanoe.	
1812	**1812**
June: Tecumseh moves north to Canada to join the British against the Americans.	Hudson's Bay Company founds the Red River Settlement.
July 12: General William Hull invades Canada from Fort Detroit.	

Tecumseh and His Times

Canada and the World

August 13: General Isaac Brock and Tecumseh meet for the first time.

August 16: Brock and Tecumseh capture Detroit.

October 13: General Brock killed at Battle of Queenston Heights.

1813
January 22: British and Indian allies defeat Americans at Battle of Frenchtown, on the River Raisin just south of Detroit.

January 23: River Raisin Massacre in which thirty American prisoners at Frenchtown are murdered by Indians, but Tecumseh not present.

Spring/summer: Tecumseh and the British twice lay siege to Fort Meigs in Ohio, but fail to capture it.

1813
March 27: Oliver Hazard Perry arrives at Presque Isle, Pennsylvania, to begin building a U.S. Navy fleet on Lake Erie.

April 27: Americans capture York (Toronto).

June: Laura Secord makes her historic twenty-mile walk to warn of a surprise American attack.

Tecumseh and His Times   **Canada and the World**

September 10: American ships
defeat the British in Battle of
Lake Erie, clearing the way for
an invasion of Canada.

September 27: British
general Henry Procter begins
retreat up the Thames River
from Amherstburg, despite
Tecumseh's objections.

Late September: Harrison
and his army sail across Lake
Erie and land at Amherstburg
to pursue the British and
Tecumseh.

October 4: General
Procter decides to make a
stand against Harrison at
Moraviantown, along the
Thames River.

October 5: Tecumseh dies at
the Battle of the Thames.

1814
August 24–25: British/
Canadians burn Washington.

Tecumseh and His Times	*Canada and the World*
	December 24: War of 1812 ends with the Peace of Ghent.
	1815 January 11: John A. Macdonald, destined to become the first prime minister of Canada, is born.
	February 17: Treaty of Ghent ratified, officially ending the war between the United States and British Canada.
	1818 The 49th parallel becomes Canada–U.S. border from Lake of the Woods to the Rocky Mountains.
1836 Tenskwatawa, the Prophet, moves out West after the Battle of the Thames and dies in obscurity.	
1840 Soldier/writer John Richardson, who fought alongside Tecumseh,	

Tecumseh and His Times	*Canada and the World*

attempts to find Tecumseh's grave, but cannot find the battleground where he was killed.

Autumn: William Henry Harrison elected ninth president of the United States.

1841
April 4: President Harrison dies on his thirty-second day in office, beginning what becomes known as Tecumseh's Curse.

1843
Paukeesau, Tecumseh's son who lived in obscurity after his father's death, dies in a village somewhere west of the Mississippi River.

1860
Abraham Lincoln elected sixteenth president of the United States.

1865
April 14: Lincoln assassinated, becoming the second

Tecumseh and His Times	**Canada and the World**

president elected in a year
ending in zero to die in office.

1880
James Garfield, twentieth
American president, elected.

1881
September 19: President
Garfield, shot by an assassin
in July, dies of infection. He
becomes the third president
elected in a year ending in
zero to die in office.

1900
William McKinley re-elected
president.

1901
September 14: McKinley dies
of complications eight days
after being shot by an assassin.

1920
Warren Harding elected
twenty-ninth president of the
United States.

Tecumseh and His Times	*Canada and the World*

1923

August 2: Harding dies in office of natural causes, the fifth presidential death attributed to Tecumseh's Curse.

1930s

Public notice over Tecumseh's Curse grows when *Ripley's Believe or Not* takes note of it.

1940

Franklin D. Roosevelt re-elected as president of the United States.

1945

April 12: President Roosevelt dies in office of natural causes.

1960

John F. Kennedy elected thirty-fifth president of the United States.

1963

November 22: Kennedy assassinated in Dallas, seventh

Tecumseh and His Times	*Canada and the World*

president elected in a year
ending in zero to die in office.

1989

President Ronald Reagan
leaves office, the first
American president elected in
well over one hundred years
not to die in office after being
elected or re-elected in a year
ending in zero. He was shot
by a would-be assassin early
in his first term, but survived.

2009

January: George W. Bush
leaves office after two terms as
American president. He was
elected in 2000, and people
believing in Tecumseh's Curse
see this as the end of the curse.

Sources Consulted

Drake, Benjamin. *Life of Tecumseh, and of His Brother the Prophet*. Cincinnati: E. Morgan Company, 1841. (Available at *www.pgdp.net.*)

Edmunds, R. David. *Tecumseh and the Quest for Indian Leadership*. Boston: Little Brown and Company, 1984.

Edmunds, R. David. *The Shawnee Prophet*. Lincoln: University of Nebraska, 1983.

Stephen Ruddell and Tecumseh. *Letters of John Mulherin Ruddell to Lyman Copeland Draper*. *Virginia Genealogist* Vol. 27, No. 4.

Goltz, H.C.W. *Dictionary of Canadian Biography Online*. Toronto/Laval: University of Toronto/Université Laval, 2000. *www.biographi.ca.*

Hatch, William Stanley. *A Chapter of the History of the War of 1812 in the Northwest*. Cincinnati: Miami Printing Publishing Co., 1872.

Heckewelder, John. *History, Manners, and Customs of the Indian Nations Who Once Inhabited Pennsylvania and the Neighboring States*. Philadelphia: Historical Society of Pennsylvania, 1876.

Hitsman, J. Mackay. *The Incredible War of 1812: A Military History*. Toronto: University of Toronto Press, 1965.

Hoxie, Frederick E., ed. *Encyclopedia of North American Indians: Native American History, Culture, and Life from Paleo-Indians to the Present*. Boston: Houghton Mifflin Harcourt, 1996.

Klinck, C.F. *Tecumseh: Fact and Fiction in Early Records*. Ottawa: Tecumseh Press, 1978.

Lossing, Benson J. *Pictorial Field-Book of the War of 1812*. Gretna, LA: Pelican Publishing Company, 2001.

Raymond, Ethyl T. *Tecumseh: A Chronicle of the Last Great Leader of His People*. Toronto: Glasgow, Brook and Company, 1920.

Reynolds, James. *Journal of an American Prisoner at Fort Malden and Quebec in the War of 1812*. Project Gutenberg EBook, *www.gutenberg.org/etext/26518*.

Richardson, John. *Richardson's War of 1812*. Toronto: Historical Publishing Co., 1902.

Ruddell, Stephen. *Reminiscences of Tecumseh's Youth*. Wisconsin Historical Society, Document No. AJ-155, *www.wisconsinhistory.org/turningpoints/search.asp?id=260*.

Schmalz, Peter S. *The Ojibwa of Southern Ontario*. Toronto: University of Toronto Press, 1991.

St. Denis, Guy. *Tecumseh's Bones*. Montreal and Kingston, ON: McGill-Queen's University Press, 2005.

Sugden, John. *Tecumseh: A Life*. New York: Henry Holt and Company, 1997.

Sugden, John. *Tecumseh's Last Stand*. Oklahoma: University of Oklahoma Press, 1985.

Taylor, Alan. *The Divided Ground: Indians, Settlers, and the Northern Borderland of the American Revolution*. New York: Knopf, 2006.

Trial of Brigadier-General William Hull, The. Pamphlet. Library of Congress, 1814.

Tupper, Ferdinand Brock. *The Life and Correspondence of Major-General Isaac Brock KB.* Guersney, U.K.: H. Redstone, 1847.

Turner, Frederick. *The Portable North American Indian Reader.* New York: Viking Press, 1974.

Vercheres de Boucherville, Thomas. *War on the Detroit: The Chronicles of Thomas Vercheres de Boucherville.* Chicago: The Lakeside Press, 1940.

Index

Albany, New York, 113
Amherstburg, 96–102, 104, 107
Appalachian Mountains, 10, 17,
    18, 21, 23, 36, 39, 41, 49,
    168, 170
Auglaize River, 51, 77

Baby, Jean Baptiste, 100, 102
Barclay, Captain Robert Heriot,
    134, 133–36, 140, 142
Barron, Joseph, 79
Bass Islands, 133, 135–37
Beaver Wars, 18, 165
"Big Fish" (*see* Ruddell, Stephen)
Big Rock, Ohio, 46
Blue Jacket, Chief, 48, 54, 56, 57,
    75, 172
Boone, Daniel, 52
Brant, Joseph (Thayendanegea),
    51, 155, 176
Brock, General Isaac, 99, *103*,
    104–15, 119–21, 127, 132,
    138, 157, 164, 168, 178, 187

Brock University, 120
Brownstown, Battle of, 98, 101,
    102, 104, 131
Brownstown Creek, 101
Buchanan's Station, 44, 45, 173
Bush, George W., 13, 184

Caldwell, Captain William, 149
Campbell, Major William, 55, 120
Canard River (Rivière aux
    Canards), 100, 101, 143
Chatham, Ontario, 9, 142–45
Chattanooga, Tennessee, 41, 43,
    173
Chauncey, Commodore Isaac, 130
Cheeseekau (brother), 16, 24,
    28, 31, 33–35, 39–45, 167,
    171, 172
Chickamauga (Cherokee), 41–43,
    62
Chickamauga War, 40
Chickasaw, 9, 41, 53, 58, 59, 87
Chillicothe, 18, 60, 61, 75, 160, 176

Choctow, 9, 53, 87
Clark, George Rogers, 31
Clay, General Green, 123, 127
Cumberland River, 41–44
Custer's Last Stand, 48

Deer Creek, 58
Delawares, 39, 40, 49, 51, 58, 71
Denny, Major Ebenezer, 48
Detroit River, 96, 97, 99, 101,
    110, 131, 138, 155
Dickson, James, 9, 10, 14
Donne, John, 161
Dragging Canoe (Tsi-yu-guns-
    ni), 41
Dudley, Colonel William
    (Dudley's Defeat), 124, 126
Dunmore, Lord, 25

Elliott, Captain Matthew, 143, 149
Erie, Lake (Battle of), 134, 179

Fallen Timbers (Battle of), 54,
    56, 66, 173, 174
Fort Dearborn, 119
Fort Detroit, 32, 49, 50, 95, 98,
    99, 101, 108–10, 112, 113,
    116, 119, 121, 140, 158, 164,
    177, 178, 187
Fort Malden, 98, 99, 138, 139,
    143, 186
Fort Meigs, 119, 121, 123, 124,
    126–28, 131, 178
Fort Miami, 55, 56, 120, 124, 138
Fort Michilimackinac, 32, 102, 119
Fort Niagara, 32

Fort Recovery, 53, 54, 56
Fort Stephenson, 128
Fort Washington (Cincinnati),
    48, 53
Fort Wayne, Treaty of, 77, 82, 83,
    176
Frenchtown (Michigan), 121,
    122, 178

Garfield, James, 10, 182
Ghent, Treaty of, 180
Gist, Christopher, 18, 19
Gist, Thomas, 27
Glaize (village), 51, 53–55, 58
Glegg, Major John, 107, 109
Great Miami River, 29, 58
Greenville (Ohio), Treaty of, 56,
    57, 73–75
Grosse Isle, 131, 144

Handley, Captain Samuel, 45
Handsome Lake, 70
Hardin, Colonel John, 47
Harding, Warren, 10, 182, 183
Harmar, General Josiah, 47, 48, 172
Harrison, William Henry, 10, 12,
    56, 57, 66, 67, 72, 74, 77, 89–
    92, 94, 95, 116, 118, 120–24,
    126, 127, 131, 132, 136, 137,
    142, 144–50, 154, 156–58,
    162, 174, 176, 177, 179, 181;
    nickname, 157
Hartley's Point, Ontario, 142
Hatch, Colonel William Stanley,
    61, 185
Heckewelder, John, 32, 65, 185

Herrod, Thomas, 60
Hokoleskwa, Chief (Cornstalk), 25
Hull, General William, 99, 102, 104,
    107–09, 116, 113, 177, 187
Hunting, 15, 17, 20, 22, 31, 35,
    36, 39, 52, 66, 75

Illinois Territory, 77
Indian Territory, 32, 60, *67*
Indiana Territory, 66, 72, 77, 85,
    174, 177
Iroquois (Six Nations), 18, 22, 23,
    25, 38, 49, 70, 165, 166, 168

Johnson, Colonel Richard
    Mentor, 146, 148, 150–57
Johnson, James, 150

Kennedy, John F., 12, 183
Kirker, Thomas, 75
Kenton, Simon, 52, 53, 59, 61
Kethtippecanoogi (*see*
    Tippecanoe)
King George III of Britain, 18,
    21, 23
Kispoko (Shawnee tribe), 16, 17
Knoxville, 45

Lalawéthika (*see* Tenskwatawa)
Lawrence, Captain James, 135
Lincoln, Abraham, 10, 181
Little Miami River, 29, 31
Little Turtle, Chief, 48, 54, 172
Long Knives, 23, 25, 26, 36, 43,
    49, 54, 85, 91, 94, 97, 101
Lookout Mountain, 43

Lorimier, Louis, 39, 40

Madison, James, 77, 114
Mad River, 29, 31, 32, 35, 170
Maguaga, Battle of, 101, 102, 119
Mamate (wife), 64
Maumee River, 51, 54, 55, 119,
    120, 123, 124, 173
McGregor's Creek, Ontario, 145
McKinley, William, 10, 182
Methoataaskee (mother), 16, 18,
    24, 29–31, 45, 167
Miamis, 49, 51, 76, 78, 82, 90
Michigan Territory, 21, 100, 101,
    112, 122, 131, 156, 171
Mill Creek (Tennessee), 44
Mingos, 25, 54
Moluntha, Chief, 36
Montcalm, Marquis de, 20
Moravian Church, 145
Moraviantown, 145–48, 150, 158,
    163, 179
Muscogee Indians (Creek), 10

Naywash, Chief, 156
New Madrid earthquake, 10, 43, 93
Niagara, 119–20, 127, 129, 140, 146
Niagara Falls, 115

Ohio Company, 19–21
Ohio River, 17, 18, 19, 23, 26, 37,
    47, 49, 115, 165
Ohio Territory (Ohio Country),
    17–22, 26, 27, *30*, 32, 38, 51,
    56, 115, 133, 166, 168, 170
Ojibwe (*Ojibway, Ojibwa*), 7, 49, 54

"Our Father with One Arm" (*see* Barclay, Robert)

Owen, Colonel Abraham, 91

Paris, Treaty of, 21, 49, 167

Paukeesau (son), *63*, 64, 149, 158

Perry, Master Commandant Oliver Hazard, 130, 132, 135–37, 143, 145, 178

Point Pleasant, Battle of, 25, 26, 28, 29, 45, 54, 169

Pontiac's Rebellion, 49–51, 155, 167, 168

Potawatomis Nation, 49, 54, 78

Presque Isle (Erie, Pennsylvania), 129–31, 178

Prevost, Lady, 158

Prevost, Sir George, 108, 158

Prophet, The (*see* Tenskwatawa)

Prophetstown, 76, 78, 83, 85–90, 92–94, 121, 176, 177

Pukeshinwau (father), 16–18, 23, 26, 28, 29, 167, 169; death, 28

Reagan, Ronald, 12, 13, 184

Redcoats, 101–02, 110, 120, 122, 123, 124, 138–39, 143, 146, 150

Reynolds, James, 112, 186

Richardson, John, 13, 27, 110, 111, 139, 148, 180, 186

River Raisin, 101, 102, 111, 121, 122, 142, 150, 178

Rivière aux Canards (*see* Canard River)

Roosevelt, Franklin, 12, 183

Roundhead, Chief, 114, 122, 123, 131

Ruddell, Stephen (Big Fish), 22, 28, 31, 32, 34, 35, 37, 52–54, 59, 64, 77, 185, 186

Ruddell's Station, 22

Sackett's Harbour, 130

St. Catharines, Ontario, 120

St. Clair River, 14, 143, 145, 153

St. Clair, General Arthur, 48, 49, 53, 54, 91, 172

Sandusky, Ohio, 128, 137

Sandwich (Windsor), 99, 100, 102, 109, 143, 144

Sauawaseekau (brother), 16, 54, 55

Scalping, 26–28, 34, 41, 110, 130, 153

Scioto River, 17, 18, 23, 26, 29, 30, 46, 60, 169

Scioto Valley, 17

Shane, Anthony, 153

Shawtunte (Richard Sparks), 17, 29

Shelby, Governor Isaac, 146

Sherman, William Tecumseh, 160

Simcoe, John Graves, 161, 175

Sparks, Richard (*see* Shawtunte)

Swan Creek, 55, 56

Tamanend, Chief, 162

Tecumapease (sister), 16, 31, 33, 64, 144, 158

Tecumseh, appearance, 61–62, 64, 81, 106, 107, 115–16; birth, 16; character, 34, 37, 46, 64, 80, 106, 114–15, 125, 139,

161–62, 164; childhood, 22,
23–24, 28, 33–35; death, 44,
151–53, *163*; family, 16–18,
29–31, 44, 62–64; as hunter,
35, 40, 52, 66; as leader, 46,
59–60, 65, 75–76, 79, 86,
93, 115, 164; meets Brock,
105–06, *106*, 108; monuments
to, 160, 162–63; naming
ceremony, 16; as warrior, 34,
35, 37, 42, 44–46, 53–55, 61,
88, 97, 101–02, 110–11, 125,
148, 162; wives, 62–64

Tecumseh's Curse, 9–13, 157–58

Tennessee River, 40–42, 171

Tenskwatawa (The Prophet,
Lalawéthika) (brother), *11*,
12, 29, 54, 62, 68–74, 76,
78–81, 86, 89–92, *121*, 158,
169, 175, 176, 180, 185

Terre Haute, Indiana, 121

Thames River (Battle of), 9, 27, 84,
111, 140, 142, 148, 151, *152*,
153–58, 160, 163, 179, 180

Thayendanegea (*see* Brant, Joseph)

Tiffin, Edward, 60

Tippecanoe (Kethtippecanoogi),
76, 85, 94, 126, 157, 176, 177

Toledo, 51, 119

Toronto (*see* York)

Trafalgar, Battle of, 133, *134*, 175

Treaties, 29, 32, 49, 51, 56–57, 66,
77–79, 82, 86

Van Buren, Martin, 12, 157

Vincennes (Indiana capital), 72,

79, 80, 86, 90, 177

Waashaa Monetoo, 34, 68, 70, 73,
75, 91, 92, 96, 176

Wabash River, 48, 49, 76, 77, 79,
82, 83, 87, 89, 94, 172, 176

Wabelegunequa (White Wing), 64

Wahsikegaboe, 158

Walpole Island, 14, 153

Walton Trace, 45

Wapakoneta, Ohio, 76, 77

War of 1812, 96, 159, 164

War Department, 86, 88, 102

Washington, George, 18, 47–49,
171, 172

Waterloo, Battle of, 108

Wayne, General "Mad Anthony,"
53, 56, 173

Wellington, Duke of, 108

White River, 58, 64, 71

White Wing (*see*
Wabelegunequa)

Winchester, General James, 120,
122

Wolfe, General James, 20

Wood, Captain Eleazor, 123

York (Toronto), 99, 114, 120, 127,
129, 154, 178

Ziegler, Jacob, 43

Ziegler's Station, 42, 43, 172